Fine Filipino Food

The Hippocrene Cookbook Library

Afghan Food & Cookery
African Cooking, Best of Regional
Albanian Cooking, Best of
Argentina Cooks!
Australia, Good Food From
Austrian Cuisine, Best of, Exp. Ed.
Bavarian Cooking
Belgian Cookbook, A
Brazilian Cookery, The Art of
Bulgarian Cooking, Traditional
Burma, Flavors of,
Cajun Women: Recipes & Remembrances from South Louisiana Kitchens, Cooking With
Caucasus Mountains, Cuisines of the
Croatian Cooking, Best of, Exp. Ed.
Czech Cooking, Best of, Exp. Ed.
Danube, All Along The, Exp. Ed.
Dutch Cooking, Art of, Exp. Ed.
Egyptian Cooking
Eritrea, Taste of
Filipino Food, Fine
Finnish Cooking, Best of
French Caribbean Cuisine
French-English Dictionary of Gastronomic Terms
French Fashion, Cooking in the (Bilingual)
Greek Cuisine, The Best of, Exp. Ed.
Haiti, Taste of
Havana Cookbook, Old (Bilingual)
Hungarian Cookbook
Hungarian Cooking, Art of, Rev. Ed.
Icelandic Food & Cookery
Indian Spice Kitchen
International Dictionary of Gastronomy
Irish-Style, Feasting Galore
Italian Cuisine, Treasury of (Bilingual)
Japanese Home Cooking
Korean Cuisine, Best of
Laotian Cooking, Simple
Latvia, Taste of

Lithuanian Cooking, Art of
Mayan Cooking
Mongolian Cooking, Imperial
Norway, Tastes and Tales of
Persian Cooking, Art of
Peru, Tastes of
Poland's Gourmet Cuisine
Polish Cooking, Best of, Exp. Ed.
Polish Country Kitchen Cookbook
Polish Cuisine, Treasury of (Bilingual)
Polish Heritage Cookery, Ill. Ed.
Polish Traditions, Old
Portuguese Encounters, Cuisines of
Pyrenees, Tastes of
Quebec, Taste of
Rhine, All Along The
Romania, Taste of, Exp. Ed.
Russian Cooking, Best of, Exp. Ed.
Scandinavian Cooking, Best of
Scotland, Traditional Food From
Scottish-Irish Pub and Hearth Cookbook
Sephardic Israeli Cuisine
Sicilian Feasts
Slovak Cooking, Best of
Smorgasbord Cooking, Best of
South African Cookery, Traditional
South American Cookery, Art of
South Indian Cooking, Healthy
Spanish Family Cookbook, Rev. Ed.
Sri Lanka, Exotic Tastes of
Swiss Cookbook, The
Syria, Taste of
Taiwanese Cuisine, Best of
Thai Cuisine, Best of, Regional
Turkish Cooking, Art of
Turkish Cuisine, Taste of
Ukrainian Cuisine, Best of, Exp. Ed.
Uzbek Cooking, Art of
Wales, Traditional Food From
Warsaw Cookbook, Old

Fine Filipino Food

Karen Hulene Bartell

HIPPOCRENE BOOKS
NEW YORK

Also by Karen Hulene Bartell:
The Best of Korean Cuisine
The Best of Taiwanese Cuisine
The Best of Polish Cooking

641.59599

Book and jacket design by Acme Klong Design, Inc.

For more information, address:
HIPPOCRENE BOOKS, INC.
171 Madison Avenue
New York, NY 10016

ISBN 0-7818-0964-9
Cataloging-in-Publication Data available from the Library of Congress.
Printed in the United States of America.

Contents

5

This book is dedicated with love to Peter Bartell,
my travel buddy, best friend, and husband.

Special thanks to Taiji and our Filipino friends from St. Christopher's in Taipei,
Taiwan, who introduced us to the incomparable cuisine of the Philippines.

Fine Filipino Food

The purpose of this cookbook is to introduce Americans to the myriad of cooking methods and exotic fare that compose Filipino[1] cuisine. One obstacle to experimenting with ethnic cuisines is finding the ingredients. To make the cooking and shopping processes easier, food substitutions are suggested throughout this book and on page 19, and ethnic grocery store locations are listed in the back under Sources for Filipino Ingredients.

Filipino cuisine has a broad base. Thanks to the Philippines' location, it is blessed with abundant natural food sources: seafood, fruits, vegetables, and wild game. Because the 7,100 islands compose an archipelago, the sea is a principal source of food. When the freshwater fish in rivers, brooks, roadside canals, and flooded rice fields are included, it is easy to see why fish, crustaceans, and other sea creatures are the basis of Filipino diets.

Milkfish or *bangus*, a bony fish with a subtle flavor, is popular in the Philippines. (It is available frozen in Filipino or Asian markets.) Tilapia, catfish, and squid are common Filipino foods that are found in most grocery stores. Popular Filipino shellfish include crabs, clams, oysters, and shrimp, the latter of which is traditionally prepared with the heads on. Dried and smoked fish are common, and dried anchovies are popular snacks.

Other principal food ingredients in the Filipino diet come from the land. Rice and coconut are the two major ingredients in Philippine food. Steamed, fluffy, white rice is the staple food of the Philippines. It is the basis of every meal, and it is eaten with everything. A *viand* is a dish eaten with rice. Soup dishes are accompanied by *sinigang*; bouillon, fish, and vegetables are used to flavor it. Bread and wheat are also gaining popularity, but rice is still the staple food in Filipino society despite competition from newer products.

Coconut is a recurring theme in Filipino cuisine. The tender flesh of the young coconut, *buko*, is cooked into a syrup, made into candies, added to salads, or boiled like noodles. It is the more mature coconut flesh that is grated and then pressed to yield coconut cream and milk, which are used in cooking countless dishes. Coconut oil is used for frying. *Macapuno* (preserved shredded coconut) and *nata de coco* (coconut gel) are used in sweets and desserts. The heart of the coconut palm, *ubod*, is sweet and crunchy. It can be made into *lumpia* (egg roll) by sautéing with shrimp or pork, then wrapping in a thin crepe.

---

[1] Filipino and Philippine are both adjectives relating to the Philippines, its people, and its culture. The two terms are used interchangeably here.

Many Filipino cakes and delicacies use cassava flour or sweet rice flour. Tapioca pearls and agar-agar (gelatin extracted from seaweed) are used to make desserts such as *sago*.

Noodles are nearly as popular as rice in the Philippines. Many varieties of noodles are available: *bihon* (rice stick noodles), *canton* (Chinese wheat noodles), *mami* (wide Chinese egg noodles), *miki* (flat egg noodles), *misua* or *miswa* (angel hair pasta), *sotanghon* (transparent bean or cellophane noodles), and *udon* (wide Japanese noodles). Most, if not all, are available at Asian markets.

Vegetables grow in the Philippines in abundance year-round. Usually they are simply steamed and enjoyed for their natural flavor. Sometimes they are tossed with vinegar, which constitutes the native salad. Several local vegetables can be difficult to find outside of the Philippines, such as *kangkong* (water spinach or swamp cabbage) or *saluyot* (jute leaves). (See Substitutions on page 19.) Gourds such as *upo* (winter melon) are used as a vegetable when tender and immature and as a bathing sponge when dried. Okra, Philippine eggplant, yard-long beans, lima beans, tomatoes, onions, bitter melon, and potatoes are basics. Purple yam, taro, cassava, and sweet potatoes are used both as vegetables and sweet fillings for pastries.

Fruits such as papaya, mango, and plantain are also eaten as vegetables, especially with *bagoong* or rock salt when green. When fruits are ripe, they are considered desserts or snacks. Tropical fruits are plentiful: jackfruit, guava, star fruit, sweetsop, chico, plantains, and bananas. There are many varieties of bananas: the *saba* for cooking, the small sweet *latundan*, the larger exportable *bongolan*, the red-skinned *morado*, the seed-filled *Espanola*, the slim, finger-like *senoritas*, and the *saging*, which is similar to plantains. No part of the banana is wasted. *Puso ng saging*, banana heart or blossom, is prepared with coconut milk. Banana leaves are used as wrappers for steaming foods.

No Filipino meal is complete without sour, sweet, and salty condiments. These flavors go well beyond mere vinegar and salt. Many green fruits provide the sour power: tamarind, green mango, and green guava, as well as *calamansi* (a tiny, sour citrus that looks like a miniature lime) or *kamias* (a sour native fruit). The sweet flavor comes from sugar (palm, white, raw, or brown) or fruit juice (orange, pineapple, sweet guava, sweet mango, papaya, or rambutan, a close cousin of the lychee). Sauces provide the salt. The most popular salty flavorings are *bagoong*, a fermented fish or seafood paste; *patis*, a combination of fish and shrimp fermented sauces; and *buro*, a fermented rice and fish sauce. Soy sauce and vinegar are the Filipino staples. Vinegar comes in many flavors: pineapple, coconut, sago palm, and sugar cane.

The first meat in the Philippines was wild game: deer and wild boar. Later domesticated animals, such as the *carabao* (water buffalo), chicken, pig, and goat, made their way into the Filipino diet. Again simplicity is the key to preparing meats. Simmering in broth and grilling over coals remain the favorite cooking methods.

Due to its versatility and comparatively low price, pork is popular; all parts of the pig are used. Beef is an expensive but primary source of protein in southern Mindanao, where the Islamic influence reduces the pork consumption. Various sausages such as Chinese *lup cheong*, Spanish *chorizo*, and Filipino *longanisa* are eaten for breakfast or added to flavor dishes. Goat meat and even stuffed frogs are eaten in certain regions.

The Philippine Islands are at a crossroads of shipping lanes. As a result, many cultures have influenced Filipino cuisine. An early foreign influence came from the Chinese, who began trading with the Philippines as early as the ninth century. They introduced stir-frying, deep-frying, noodles, and soy products. The Chinese influence is easy to find: soy sauce, tofu, and other soybean products, as well as vegetables, such as *petsay*, *toge* (mung bean sprouts), *mustasa* (pickled mustard greens), Chinese black dried mushrooms, *daikon* (white radish), *bok choy*, bamboo shoots, Chinese celery, water chestnuts, and lemongrass.

Filipino cooks incorporated the new Chinese cooking methods but added their own indigenous ingredients. As a result, *pancit* (sautéed noodles) are not complete without a twist of fresh *calamansi*, and *lumpia* (the Filipino answer to spring rolls) have their own unique Filipino variation: a dipping sauce of crushed garlic and vinegar.

Malaysian spice traders brought seasonings from the Spice Islands and introduced that delectable appetizer, satay.

Spanish colonization from 1521 to 1898 brought with it a new cuisine. Along with the Spanish influence came Mexican flavors since the Philippines was, at that time, governed through Mexico. The Spanish introduced a range of ingredients and dishes from the Iberian Peninsula, as well as North, Central, and South America: olive oil, wine, and European seasonings, as well as tomatoes, potatoes, corn, and chocolate. They used such cooking methods as sautéing and stewing in oil and wine. Even today, many Filipino dishes are based on garlic, onions, and tomatoes, remnants of a Spanish influence.

However, because Spanish food emphasized meat and dairy products, which were considered luxury items, Spanish fare was viewed as upper class, fiesta cuisine, while Chinese food was considered everyday cuisine. Many Spanish-derived dishes show up on the table only at Christmas or fiesta time and are quickly identified by their Spanish names: *relleno*, *mechado*, *pochero*, *leche flan*.

Adobo, arguably the best-known Filipino dish, is a by-product of both Spanish and Chinese influence. In Spanish cuisine, *adobo* refers to a pickling sauce made from olive oil, vinegar, garlic, oregano, paprika, thyme, bay leaf, and salt. The Filipinos embraced their favorite flavors (vinegar, garlic, and bay leaf), included peppercorns, and, nodding to the Chinese influence, added soy sauce.

They then adapted it to be a stewing sauce for chicken and pork, but maintained its Spanish moniker. Once again, the Filipino palate affirmed itself.

Finally Americans came with an all-encompassing culture and cuisine. The American colonization from 1898 to 1946 impacted Philippine food, leaving the legacies of speed and convenience. Where the Spaniards had reserved education for the elite, the Americans set out to educate the entire population. Within a generation, not only did Filipinos speak English, they became consumers of American products. Prepackaged foods, canned goods, and fast-food chains are the American influences on Philippine food.

One difference between American and Filipino meals is the order of dishes served at meals. American custom calls for soup or an appetizer, followed by salad, followed by the entrée and side dishes, ending with dessert. However, Filipino custom calls for placing all the dishes on the table at the same time, with diners deciding their own combination and sequence.

Substitutions

Asian and Filipino foods are becoming more commonplace on supermarket shelves. A listing of specialty stores for Filipino ingredients in selected North American cities is also included in the back. However, if all else fails and certain ingredients are unavailable, try these substitutions.

INGREDIENT	SUBSTITUTE
Achuete, atsuete, 1 tablespoon	⅛ teaspoon red food coloring
Achuete, atsuete, 1 tablespoon used in pancit molo	2 teaspoons paprika
Bangus (milkfish)	Salmon or trout
Bulaklak ng saging	Dried lily blossoms available at Asian supermarkets
Calamansi	Lime or Lemon
Chorizo de Bilbao	Pepperoni, garlic sausage, or oxford sausage
Gabi	Yam
Kamias	Lemon juice or rhubarb
Kangkong	Watercress or spinach
Labanos	Red or white radish
Macapuno (young coconut)	Coconut
Misua	Very fine noodles (angel hair pasta)
Patis (fish sauce)	Rock salt, soy sauce and freshly squeezed lemon juice, or soy sauce and kumquats
Puso ng saging (banana hearts)	Artichoke hearts
Saluyot	Swiss chard, mustard greens
Singkamas	Turnips
Talbos ng Ampalaya	Watercress or spinach
Talbos ng sili	Spinach
Vinegars (pineapple, coconut, sago palm, sugar cane)	Apple cider vinegar, white vinegar

Filipino Cooking Methods

Binuro	Salting seafood such as *talangka* (small crabs), *alimasag* (crabs), *bangus* (milkfish), *hito* (catfish), *dalag* (mudfish), eggs, or vegetables.
Dinaing	Carving broiled or grilled fish at the back and opening like a butterfly.
Ginataan	Preparing fish, crustaceans, vegetables, or root crops in coconut milk.
Ginisa	Sautéing meat, fish, fowl, or vegetables with garlic and onions in lard.
Halabos	Preparing shellfish or crustaceans with salt and almost no water. Cooks in its own juices.
Inadobo	Preparing meat, fish, or vegetables with vinegar and spices.
Inasnan	Preserving meat, fish, or vegetables with salt. May be broiled.
Inihaw	Broiling meat, fish, or root crops over live charcoal.
Kinilaw	Marinating raw food such as seviche in vinegar and spices.
Nilaga	Simmering fish, fowl, or meat in water.
Pangat	Preparing fish with a little water, and with or without a souring agent.
Pasingao	Steaming fish, shellfish, meat, or fowl.
Pesa	Boiling sautéed fish with ginger, vegetables, and *patis*.
Pinaksiw	Preparing fish with vinegar, very little water, and spices. May be made with or without vegetables.
Pinais	Wrapping food in banana or *alagao* leaves and steaming.
Pinausukan	Smoking fish, meat, or fowl.
Sinigang	Preparing with water and adding a fruit or vegetable souring agent. Food may be meat, fish, or fowl.
Sinuam	Boiling sautéed fish or shellfish with ginger and chili pepper leaves.
Tinapa	Blanching fish and sautéing it until golden brown.

Glossary

Achara	Pickled fruits or vegetables served as relish
Adobong or **Adobo**	Cooking method; to stew meat, seafood or vegetables in vinegar, garlic and black pepper
Agar-Agar	Gelatin derived from seaweed, available in Asian food stores
Alimango	A variety of crab with large pincers
Alimasag	A smaller variety of crab than the alimango
Alugbati or **Alogbati**	A red-stemmed vine whose green leaves are used in many dishes
Ampalaya	Bitter melon
Apritada	A meat dish with tomato sauce and vegetables
Apulid	Water chestnuts
Arroz	Spanish word for *rice*
Asado	A meat dish made with tomatoes, onions, and seasonings
Atis	Sweetsop
Atsuete	Annatto
Baboy	Tagalog word for *pork* or *pig*
Bagoong	Salty, fermented paste made of shrimp or fish
Balut	Embryonated duck eggs
Bangus	Milkfish
Bayabas	Guava
Binuro	Cooking method; to use salt as a preservative
Bistek	Stir-fried steak; beefsteak
Buko	Young coconut
Calamansi	Small tropical fruit, similar to lime or lemon
Caldereta	Stew made traditionally with goat meat
Camaron rebosado	Shelled shrimp, dipped in batter, and deep-fried
Cassava	Edible, starchy root used in making bread in tapioca
Chico	Sapodilla or naseberry

Chorizo de Bilbao	Spanish sausage
Dahon ng sili	Chili pepper leaves
Dilis	Dried anchovies
Dinaing	Cooking method; to marinate butterflied fish with vinegar, then fry or broil
Dinuguan Baboy	Pork blood stew
Embutido	Ground pork roll, stuffed with pickles, eggs, and raisins
Empanada	Meat-filled pastry turnovers
Empanadita	Pastry made with honey and nuts
Ensalada	Spanish work for *salad*
Escabeche	Fish in sweet-and-sour sauce
Estofado	Stewed meat dish prepared with vinegar, sugar, and spices
Frito or **Fritong**	Cooking method; to fry
Flan	Custard prepared with milk and egg yolks
Fritada	A meat dish with tomato sauce and vegetables
Gabi	Taro
Gallina	Spanish for *chicken*
Gata	Tagalog for *coconut milk*
Guinataan or **Ginataan**	Cooking method; to cook meat, seafood, or vegetables in coconut milk
Goto	Tripe
Guinisa	Cooking method; to saute with garlic and onions
Guisado	Tagalog for *sautéed*
Gulaman	Agar-agar
Halabos	Cooking method; to steam shellfish or crustacean with little water
Hamon	Tagalog for *ham*
Hipon	Shrimp
Inasan	Cooking method; to preserve foods with salt
Inihaw	Tagalog for *charcoal-broiled*; to grill or broil
Itlog na Maalat	Salted eggs

Kabute	Mushroom
Kalabasa	Squash
Kamote	Sweet potato or yam
Kamoteng Kahoy	Cassava
Kangkong	Green vegetable indigenous to Philippines; flavor is similar to spinach; texture is similar to watercress
Kaong	Palm nuts
Kare-kare	Meat-vegetable stew with oxtail, beef, or tripe cooked in peanut sauce
Kawali	Filipino skillet
Kinchay	Chinese celery
Kilawin or **Kinilaw**	Cooking method; to marinate meat or seafood in vinegar and souring agents such as calamansi, lemon, or lime juice
Kuhol	Tagalog for *snails*
Kutsay	Tagalog for *leeks*
Labanos	White radish
Labong	Tagalog for *bamboo shoots*
Langka	Tagalog for *jackfruit*
Leche flan	*Leche* is Spanish for *milk*; a milk and egg yolk custard
Lengua	Spanish word for *tongue*
Lomo	Beef loin
Longaniza	Filipino sausage
Lumpia	Filipino egg roll
Luya	Ginger
Mangga	Tagalog for *mango*
Manggang Hilaw	Tagalog for *green mango*
Manok	Tagalog for *chicken*
Mechado	Meat containing fat inserts, simmered in tomato sauce and spices
Menudo	Diced pork and liver stew with vegetables
Merienda	Afternoon tea
Miki	Rice noodles

Misua or **Miswa**	Thin wheat noodles; angel-hair pasta
Misu	Soybean paste
Mongo	Mung beans
Morcon	Ground steak roll, stuffed with pickles, eggs, and raisins
Mustasa	Mustard greens
Nangka	Jackfruit
Nilaga	Tagalog for *boiled*; to boil meats or fish in water
Paksiw	Meat or fish cooked in vinegar, garlic, and hot peppers
Pancit	Philippine pastas
Pasingao	Cooking method; to steam fish, shellfish or meats
Pastillas	Candies made of milk and sugar
Pata	Pig hocks and pigs feet
Patis	Salty extract from fermented seafood
Pechay	Bok choy
Pesa	Meat or fish and vegetables simmered with ginger
Pinakbet	Vegetable and pork stew with bagooong alamang
Pinaksiw	Cooking method; to cook fish in vinegar with water and spices
Pinausukan	Cooking method; to smoke fish and meats for flavor
Pipino	Tagalog for *cucumber*
Penoy	Duck egg
Pochero	Combination of boiled beef, chicken, dumplings, and vegetables
Pusit	Tagalog for *squid*
Puto	Steamed rice cake
Relleno or **Rellenong**	Cooking method; to stuff chicken, fish or vegetables
Saba	Cooking banana or plaintain
Saging	Banana
Sago	Tapioca pearls
Salabat	Ginger tea
Saluyot	Okra leaves
Sampalok	Tamarind
Sigarilyas	Winged bean

Sili	Long green pepper
Singkamas	Jicama
Sinigang	Cooking method; to cook a soup of meats, fish or vegetables with sour fruit such as tamarind or lemon juice
Siomai	Dumplings
Siopao	Steamed meat buns
Sitaw or **Sitao**	Chinese string beans or yard-long beans
Sotanghon	Transparent bean or cellophane noodles
Sugpo	Giant tiger prawns
Tainga ng Baboy	Pig ears
Talaba	Tagalog for *oyster*
Talong	Tagalog for Philippine *eggplant*; long, thin and purple
Tapa	Dried meat, cured with salt and vinegar
Tausi	Black soy beans, fermented and salted
Tinapa	Cooking method; to soak smoked or salted fish in water, then pan-fry
Tinola	Meat or fish flavored with ginger
Tocino	Annatto-cured pork
Togue	Bean sprouts
Tokwa	Soy bean cake
Torrones	Egg rolls with bananas
Tubo	Sugar cane
Tulya	Freshwater clams
Turo-Turo	Filipino fast-food stands; literally, "point-point"
Ube	Purple yams
Ubod	Hearts of palm
Upo	Philippine gourd
Yema	Spanish for *egg yolk*

Christmas in the Philippines

Maligayang Pasko! Merry Christmas!

Christmas is the Filipinos' best-loved celebration. Star-shaped lanterns, called *parols* in the Filipino language Tagalog, signal the start of the Christmas season in the Philippines. As early as September, these five-pointed representations of the star of Bethlehem begin lighting up neighborhoods. Why so early? Filipinos associate the months' suffix '-ber' with Christmas, so September, October, November, and December are all considered holiday months.

Parols, the Filipino counterpart of Mexican piñatas, are beacons of hospitality hung outside doors and windows, so the cheerful light brightens the evenings and welcomes visitors. Originally the *parols* were used to light the way to the *Misa de Gallo* or the Mass of the Rooster, which is held early in the morning on Christmas Day, before the roosters crow.

Framed with bamboo or rattan, the lanterns' sides are made of translucent rice paper, tissue, or colorful cellophane. To make a lantern, string together five long pieces of bamboo to form a star; make a second star. Place five twigs or small pieces of bamboo between the two stars, so that they bow apart but are joined at the points. Apply glue to the bamboo frame and cover with tissue. Tradition calls for a candle, but to be safe place a flashlight inside the lantern.

To prepare for the holiday, many people begin a novena on December 16, known as *Misa de Aguinaldo*. They attend nine consecutive days of outdoor masses held as early as four o'clock in the morning. After each mass, Filipinos gather for the traditional *almusal* or breakfast: *salabat*, local ginger tea, and *bibingka* or flat cakes served on banana leaves and topped with brown sugar and freshly grated coconut.

Breakfast for Four
MISA DE GALLO ALMUSAL

Experiment with only the traditional *Bibingka* and *Salabat* for a quick breakfast, or try all the recipes for an unforgettable Filipino holiday brunch. For a larger group, double the recipes!

Pan de Sal—Fresh Breakfast Rolls
Tortang Talong—Egglpant Omelette
Adobong Manok—Chicken Adobo
Mango Papaya Fruit Salad
Bibingka—Flat Cake
Champorrado—Chocolate Rice Porridge
Salabat—Ginger Tea
Barako—Coffee

The nine-day pre-Christmas novena ends with midnight mass on Christmas Eve. After mass comes the *Noche Buena*, or Midnight Feast, where the traditional meal is *Arroz Caldo Con Pollo*, *Caldereta*, *Paksiw na Lechón*, hot *Tsokolate*, a native chocolate drink, *Buko* salad (a misnomer), and an endless supply of Christmas cookies.

Christmas Eve Midnight Feast
NOCHE BUENA

Arroz Caldo Con Pollo—Chicken Rice Soup with Ginger
Caldereta—Hearty Beef Stew
Paksiw na Lechón—Pork Pot Roast in Lechón Sauce
Hamon—Chinese Ham
Extra Sharp Cheddar Cheese
Buko—Coconut Salad
Yema—Egg Balls
Polvoron—Powdered Milk Candy
Christmas Cookies
Tsokolate—Rich Chocolate Drink
Tangerines
Roasted Chestnuts

Fresh Breakfast Rolls

Pan de sal *is a familiar bread roll. The Filipino version differs slightly in that it is sweeter than the regular roll and delicious when eaten warm from the oven with butter.*

Soften the yeast in 2 cups lukewarm water with 1 teaspoon sugar added. Set aside for 6 to 7 minutes.

In a bowl, mix together the remaining ⅓ cup sugar, salt, and ¼ cup oil. Add the softened yeast and 3 cups flour. Blend well, gradually adding the remaining 3 cups flour and mixing until the dough no longer sticks to the sides of the bowl.

Transfer the dough to a lightly floured board, and knead until smooth, 8 to 9 minutes.* Form the dough into a ball, and place in a lightly greased bowl. Brush the surface of the dough with the remaining 1 tablespoon oil, and cover with a damp cloth. Allow to rise in a warm place away from drafts (inside a kitchen cupboard) for 2 hours, or until the dough doubles in size.

Punch down. Roll out on a floured board to ¾-inch thickness, and cut into 1½-inch strips. Sprinkle with 1 tablespoon bread crumbs. Let rise for another 15 minutes.

Cut dough into 1½-inch pieces. Arrange on a lightly greased cookie sheet, cut side up, about 1½-inches apart. Sprinkle with the remaining 3 tablespoons bread crumbs. Let rise for 30 minutes more, or until the dough doubles again in size.

Preheat oven to 375° F. Bake the *pan de sal* for 12 to 15 minutes, or until light brown. This recipe may be halved, or freeze the leftovers.

*Tip: To knead the dough, curve your fingers over it and press down with the heels of your palms. Give the dough a quarter turn, fold it over, and push down again. Knead it until it is elastic and has a satin sheen.

Ingredients:

- 2 teaspoons dry yeast
- ⅓ cup plus 1 teaspoon sugar
- 1½ teaspoons salt
- ¼ cup plus 1 tablespoon vegetable oil
- 6 cups flour
- ¼ cup dry bread crumbs

The New Year in the Philippines

On New Year's Eve, Filipino families make as much noise as possible by lighting firecrackers, beating pans, and blowing horns or whistles until midnight. The *Media Noche* is a snack served at midnight.

Media Noche New Year's Eve Snack

Biko—Sweet Rice
Salabat—Ginger Tea

On New Year's Day, try something different. Roast a pig over hot coals and serve with traditional *Pancit*, Lumpia, and *Adobo*.

New Year's Day Dinner

Whole Suckling Pig
Pancit—Canton or Noodles Cantonese-Style
Lumpia Shrimp and Vegetable Wraps
Lumpia Sauce
Pork *Adobo*
Steamed Rice
Papaya Atsara or Green Papaya Pickles
Flan
Sweet Potato Flan
Star Fruit

SALADS

Thanks to the American influence on Filipino cuisine, salads have become a regular addition to the evening meal. With the wide variety of fruits and vegetables grown in the Philippines, salads have a diversity of ingredients that is sure to tease the palate: green mango, bitter melon, bamboo shoots, jicama, and carambola.

One difference between American and Filipino salads is the texture of salads. In the Philippines, the vegetables are first pickled, preserved, blanched, boiled, or baked. These are then tossed with fresh greens. Enjoyed for their natural flavor, vegetables are often simply tossed with vinegar, which constitutes the native salad.

Another difference is the condiments. Instead of dressings, *bagoong*, a fermented shrimp paste, or dipping sauces are served. *Bagoong* is comparable to ketchup or salt in the American home; it is served with everything. Try this simple dipping sauce over vegetables: combine equal portions of soy sauce and the juice of *calamansi*, a small native fruit similar to limes.

Baby Spinach and Sprouts Salad

6 SERVINGS

Mung bean sprouts (togue) *are rich in protein and add a subtle flavor to salads.*

Combine all the ingredients. Toss well to mix evenly. Serve chilled with the Sweet and Sour Dressing (recipe follows).

.

6 cups fresh baby spinach

½ cup sliced water chestnuts

I cup fresh mung bean sprouts

3 hard-boiled eggs, coarsely chopped

½ pound bacon, cooked crisp and well-drained

¼ cup slivered almonds

Sweet and Sour Dressing

2 CUPS

Combine all the ingredients in a jar. Cover and shake well to blend.

I cup vegetable oil

¾ cup firmly packed raw or brown sugar

⅓ cup catsup

¼ cup palm or apple cider vinegar

I tablespoon Worcestershire sauce

I small onion, minced

¼ teaspoon salt, or to taste

Green Mango Salad

Immature mangoes have a piquant flavor completely unlike the sweet succulence of ripe mangoes. Experience this salad made from the green Queen of Philippine fruit.

Combine all the ingredients and toss lightly. Divide among four iced salad plates.

2 cups peeled and chopped green mango

2 cups diced plum tomatoes

1/4 cup chopped fresh cilantro

I cup finely sliced green onions

4 hard-boiled eggs, shelled and chopped

I teaspoon raw or brown sugar

1/2 teaspoon salt, or to taste

1/4 teaspoon ground black pepper, or to taste

Bitter Melon Salad

Bitter melon is available in Asian supermarkets, or substitute fresh watercress or baby spinach.

Cut the bitter melon in half lengthwise; discard the white pith and red seeds. Dice only the green skin and outer membrane. Measure 1 cup. Macerate the diced melon with 1 tablespoon salt and squeeze out the bitter juice. Then wash well under running water, squeeze dry, and place in a chilled salad bowl.

Add the shrimp and onion. Combine the vinegar, olive oil, sugar, pepper, and additional salt, if desired. Drizzle over the salad. Toss well to coat evenly. Refrigerate until ready to serve. Garnish with tomato and egg wedges.

1 (1-pound) slice bitter melon

1 tablespoon sea salt, or to taste

½ cup cooked, minced shrimp

1 large onion, minced

1 tablespoon apple cider vinegar

3 tablespoons olive oil

½ tablespoon raw or brown sugar

¼ teaspoon ground white pepper, or to taste

1 tomato, cut into wedges

2 hard-boiled eggs, peeled and cut into wedges

Bitter Melon and Green Onion Salad

Bagoong, *also know as anchovy or shrimp paste, is a salty, fermented paste that is a popular Filipino condiment. If it is not readily available, look in Asian supermarkets or substitute 2 tablespoons soy sauce and 2 tablespoons lemon juice.*

2 tablespoons salt

4 cups seeded and julienned bitter melon

I cup finely sliced green onions

¼ cup bagoong

8 medium plum tomatoes, thinly sliced

Sprinkle the salt over the bitter melon and toss well to coat the melon evenly. Place in a colander and drain for 20 minutes. Rinse thoroughly and drain again. (Salt removes some of the bitterness.)

Toss the melon with the green onions and *bagoong*. Distribute among four iced salad bowls, placing a mounded scoop in the center of each bowl. Divide the tomato slices among the bowls, arranging the slices around the mounded melon.

Bamboo Shoots and Sweet Potato Salad

6 SERVINGS

Cook the sweet potatoes the day before serving. Then toss this salad together in five minutes!

Thinly slice the bamboo shoots. Toss the bamboo shoots, sweet potatoes, and onions with the dressing. Divide the mixture among six frosty salad plates. Garnish with tomato slices, and serve chilled.

3 cups canned bamboo shoots, drained

2 cups boiled peeled, cubed, and sweet potatoes, chilled

½ cup minced onion

⅓ cup prepared Thousand Island dressing

1 large plum tomato, thinly sliced

Jicama Salad

Singkamas or jicama is an acquired taste. Its flavor is so subtle, it has almost no taste of its own, but its ability to absorb other flavors and its crunchy texture are what make it popular. A white root crop that resembles a large globular potato, it is refreshing sliced, salted, and served as a snack. It is also used as a lumpia filling, but it excels as a salad. Toss with greens and a vinaigrette dressing for a crisp, light summer salad.

Toss the jicama with the greens. Divide among four chilled salad plates. Combine the vinegar, oil, sugar, salt, and pepper in a small bottle. Shake for 1 minute, or until well blended. Drizzle the dressing over the salad, or serve on the side. Garnish with green onion slivers.

I cup peeled and thinly sliced jicama

3 cups greens

I tablespoon palm or white vinegar

3 tablespoons olive oil

½ tablespoon raw or brown sugar

½ teaspoon salt, or to taste

¼ teaspoon ground white pepper, or to taste

2 green onions, diagonally sliced

Carambola-Broccoli Salad

4 SERVINGS

Carambola, also known as balimbing, gaeang, *five corners, and star fruit, is a five-sided, pale green fruit that turns yellow when ripe. Its English name comes from the shape of its cross sections: five-pointed stars. Its Tagalog name,* balimbing, *is also a popular Filipino term for a hypocrite.*

Gently toss the broccoli, carambola, onion, currants, nuts, and water chestnuts, in a large salad bowl and chill for 30 minutes. Blend the yogurt, mayonnaise, and lime juice. Fold the dressing into the salad or serve on the side. Serve immediately in frosted salad bowls.

2 cups broccoli florets

½ cup thinly sliced carambola

¼ cup thinly sliced red onion

¼ cup currants or raisins

¼ cup macadamia nuts

2 tablespoons thinly sliced water chestnuts

2 tablespoons vanilla yogurt

2 tablespoons mayonnaise

1 teaspoon freshly squeezed lime juice

FRUIT SALADS

Fruit grows year-round in the Philippines and forms the basis for many native dishes. Tropical fruits are plentiful and varied: guava, jackfruit, star fruit, chico, sweetsop, plantains, and various varieties of bananas. Mango and papaya are eaten ripe or green.

Coconut permeates Filipino cuisine. *Macapuno* (preserved shredded coconut) and *nata de coco* (coconut gel) are used in many of the Filipino fruit salads, which can be so sweet that they may be considered desserts.

The American influence in the 1940s, with the widespread distribution of canned goods, resulted in inspired dishes. One of the happiest blends of cultures and cuisines is Filipino fruit salad, which consists of canned fruit cocktail mixed with native fruit preserves, such as *buko*, *kaong* (palm nuts), or *langka* (jackfruit), giving the canned goods a Filipino taste and texture.

Mango Papaya Fruit Salad

4 SERVINGS

Combine mango, papaya, strawberry halves, melon balls, and banana; toss lightly, and chill for 30 minutes.

In a large bowl, blend the mayonnaise and orange concentrate. Fold in the coconut and whipped topping. Fold the fruit into the dressing and toss gently. Spoon individual servings onto beds of loose-leaf lettuce. Slice the whole strawberries into thin strips. Garnish each plate with the berry slices arranged in the shape of a fan.

1 mango, peeled and pitted

1 cup peeled and cubed papaya

1 cup halved fresh strawberries

1 cup honeydew melon balls

1 banana, sliced

1/3 cup mayonnaise

1 tablespoon orange juice concentrate

2 tablespoons grated toasted fresh coconut

1/3 cup prepared whipped topping

2 cups loose-leaf lettuce

4 large strawberries

Five-Minute Coconut Salad

BUKO I   8 SERVINGS

What could be easier than a recipe that calls for only three ingredients? Look for lychees and canned coconut in Asian supermarkets.

Combine the lychees with the undrained coconut in a medium bowl. Fold in cream. Refrigerate for 1 hour before serving.	**3 (11-ounce) cans whole lychees, quartered** **6 (3.5-ounce) cans canned grated coconut in syrup** **1 cup heavy cream**

Coconut Salad

BUKO II   8 SERVINGS

Filipino ingredients are available in Asian supermarkets.

Drain the *buko*, fruit cocktail, *mata de coco*, and *kaong* thoroughly; combine in a medium bowl. Add the milk and cream, mixing well. Cover and refrigerate for at least 4 hours or overnight. Stir well before serving.	**8 ounces frozen shredded buko (young coconut), thawed** **8 ounces fruit cocktail** **1 (15-ounce) jar *mata de coco* (coconut gel)** **1 (12-ounce) jar *kaong* (palm fruit in syrup)** **1 (8-ounce) can sweetened condensed milk** **1 (8-ounce) can Nestle cream (thick, sweet topping) or 8 ounces vanilla yogurt**

Fruit Salad, Philippine-Style

12 SERVINGS

You will find lychees and macapuno *in Asian supermarkets.*

Carefully slice the pineapples lengthwise into quarters, including the green tops. Remove core. Scoop out the fruit and cut into chunks. Set aside. Wrap the shells in plastic wrap and refrigerate.

Blend the heavy cream and cheese to a smooth consistency. Toss with the fruit cocktail, pineapple chunks, lychees, *macapuno* balls, almonds, and apples, and blend well. Chill overnight. Serve spooned into the quartered pineapple shells.

3 fresh pineapples

1 ½ cups heavy cream

1 (8-ounce) package cream cheese

1 (14-ounce) can fruit cocktail, drained

1 (14-ounce) can lychees, drained

1 cup preserved macapuno balls (young coconut) or 1 cup cooked kidney beans

1 (8-ounce) package unsalted almonds, chopped

1 ½ cups cubed fresh apples

Sweetened Fruit with Coconut and Ice Cream

HALO-HALO   6 SERVINGS

This fruit-salad-cum-dessert features various types of tropical fruits and preserves layered on top of one another. It is then capped with shaved ice, and condensed milk is poured over all. It is typically served in a tall glass to better enjoy the colorful presentation. Halo-halo *roughly translates to "mix-mix," the idea being that the lucky diner stirs up the layered contents before eating. Experiment with different combinations, such as sweet beans, purple yams, jackfruit, tapioca, and various fruits. To classify this salad as a dessert beyond a shadow of a doubt, top with a scoop of ice cream or a sliver of* leche *flan. Look for* kaong, macapuno, *and* Avoset Cream *in Asian supermarkets.*

Drain the fruit cocktail and *kaong* or pineapple. Divide the ingredients among six tall glasses; layer the fruit cocktail, *kaong*, and *macapuno*. Cap each glass with shaved ice. Just before serving, pour the Avoset Cream and condensed milk over all. If desired, garnish with any combination of grated cheese, ice cream, or *leche* flan.

1 (14-ounce) can fruit cocktail

1 cup *kaong* (palm fruit in syrup) or 1 cup fresh-packed pineapple

1 (15-ounce) bottle sweetened *macapuno* (young coconut) or ½ cup sweetened coconut flakes

3 cups shaved ice

1 (15-ounce) bottle Avoset Cream (light cream) or 15 ounces light cream, optional

½ cup sweetened condensed milk

6 scoops vanilla ice cream, optional

6 slivers *leche* flan, optional (see recipe page 224)

¼ cup grated cheddar cheese, optional

Mandarin Orange Salad

Drain the fruit well and mix all ingredients, except for the whipped topping. Cover and refrigerate overnight. If necessary, drain again, and fold in the whipped topping.

1 cup mandarin oranges, fresh or canned

1 cup fruit cocktail, fresh or canned

1 cup shredded coconut

1 cup pecan pieces

2 cups whipped topping

ADOBO

Adobo could very well be called the national dish of the Philippines. The stew traditionally consists of chicken and/or pork chunks simmered in soy sauce, vinegar, bay leaf, garlic, and whole peppercorns until the meats are tender. As a cooking method, it can be used for fowl, meat, fish, shellfish, or vegetables.

Adobo is a famous Filipino *ulam* or main dish, not only because of its piquant flavor, but also because of its longevity and resilience to spoilage, an important point in the days before refrigeration. What is the secret ingredient? Vinegar.

Allow the vinegar to first reach the boiling point when making adobo; then lower the temperature to a simmer. Never stir the vinegar while simmering, or it will have a "raw" vinegar taste.

When cooking in the adobo style, use ceramic, glass, stainless steel, or wrought iron saucepans—anything but aluminum, which interacts chemically with the vinegar and impairs the flavor.

Pickled Chicken Adobo, Philippine-Style

4 TO 6 SERVINGS

Substitute one pound of pork chops for one pound of chicken for a richer blend of flavors.

Brown the chicken (and pork) in oil in a large, nonaluminum skillet. Add the garlic, soy sauce, white vinegar, pickling spices, Worcestershire sauce, and ¼ cup water. Bring to a boil. Cover and lower the heat; simmer for 30 to 35 minutes, or until the chicken is tender (and the pork is thoroughly cooked).

2 pounds chicken breasts, thighs, or legs

2 tablespoons vegetable oil

5 cloves garlic, minced

¼ cup soy sauce

¼ cup white vinegar

2 tablespoons pickling spices

2 tablespoons Worcestershire sauce

Philippine Chicken and Pork Adobo

6 TO 8 SERVINGS

Bay leaves (laurel) are used in the Philippines for flavoring stews and soups. If using dried bay leaves, however, be sure to remove them before serving.

Brown the chicken and pork in oil in a large, non-aluminum skillet. Add the vinegar, garlic, pepper, bay leaf, salt, soy sauce, and 1 cup water. Bring to a boil. Cover and lower the heat; simmer for 30 to 35 minutes, or until the chicken is tender and the pork is thoroughly cooked. Remove the bay leaf and serve steaming hot.

Tip: Add 2 tablespoons Worcestershire sauce to the adobo to enhance the dish's flavor.

1 (2-pound) chicken, cut into serving-size pieces

1 pound boneless pork, cut into 1½-inch cubes

2 tablespoons vegetable oil

1 cup palm or white vinegar

8 cloves garlic, minced

½ teaspoon ground black pepper, or to taste

1 bay leaf

1 tablespoon salt, or to taste

4 tablespoons soy sauce

Drunken Chicken Adobo

4 SERVINGS

Dark Filipino rum is best suited for this marinade because of its rich, hearty flavor, but white wine will also work. Substitute pork for the chicken, or experiment with a combination of both. Buko *is available at Asian supermarkets.*

Marinate the chicken in the rum, soy sauce, half the garlic, salt, pepper, and vinegar overnight, or for at least 2 hours. Remove the chicken and drain.

Sauté the chicken in 2 tablespoons oil for 8 to 10 minutes, or until golden brown. Pour off the excess oil and add the *buko* juice. Lower the heat, cover, and simmer for 10 to 12 minutes, or until the chicken is tender. Remove the chicken to a heated platter. Sauté the remaining garlic in the remaining 1 tablespoon oil, and sprinkle over the top of the adobo.

Variations:
Drunken Pork Adobo: substitute 2 pounds pork for the chicken. Be sure to cook thoroughly.

2 pounds chicken, cut into serving-size pieces

¼ cup dark Filipino rum

2 tablespoons soy sauce

12 cloves garlic, minced

1 teaspoon salt, or to taste

¼ teaspoon ground black pepper, or to taste

1 cup apple cider vinegar

3 tablespoons vegetable oil

1 cup *buko* juice (coconut water)

Deep-Fried Chicken Adobo

4 SERVINGS

In a nonaluminum saucepan, combine the chicken, vinegar, soy sauce, garlic, and ½ teaspoon each of the salt and pepper. Bring to a boil, cover, lower the heat, and simmer. When the liquid evaporates, add ½ cup water, and continue cooking for 12 to 15 minutes, or until the chicken is tender.

Remove the chicken from the pan and set aside. Strain the remaining adobo sauce and set aside. Bone the chicken and cut into serving-size pieces.

Combine the flour, cornstarch, and the remaining ½ teaspoon each salt and pepper. Dip chicken pieces in the egg white. Then dredge them in the dry ingredients. Sauté the chicken in hot oil for 2 to 3 minutes per side, or until crisp and golden brown. Serve with Adobo Dip (recipe follows).

2 pounds chicken thighs or breasts

½ cup palm or white vinegar

2 tablespoons soy sauce

9 cloves garlic, minced

1 teaspoon salt, or to taste

1 teaspoon ground black pepper, or to taste

½ cup flour

½ cup cornstarch

1 egg white, lightly beaten

3 tablespoons vegetable oil

Adobo Dip

1 ⅓ CUPS

Combine the adobo sauce with the mayonnaise, parsley, and garlic. Serve at room temperature as a dipping sauce for the Deep-Fried Chicken Adobo.

¼ cup adobo sauce (reserved from the Deep-Fried Chicken Adobo, above)

1 cup mayonnaise

2 tablespoons minced fresh parsley

1 teaspoon minced garlic

Marinated Chicken and Pork Adobo

8 SERVINGS

Filipinos frequently combine chicken and pork. The two white meats complement each other, offering subtle nuances of flavor found in neither individually. Taste for yourself!

In a 2-quart, nonaluminum saucepan, combine ½ cup water with the vinegar, half of the garlic, pepper, bay leaf, salt, soy sauce, and pork. Bring to a boil, then lower the heat, cover, and simmer for 25 to 30 minutes. Add the chicken, cover, and simmer for an additional 25 to 30 minutes. Add more water, if necessary.

When the pork is thoroughly cooked, and the chicken is tender, remove them from the sauce and set aside. In a skillet, sauté the remaining garlic with the vegetable oil for 1 to 2 minutes, or until golden brown. Add the meat and sauté for 5 to 7 minutes, or until lightly browned.

Return the meat and juices to the sauce. Simmer for 7 to 9 minutes, or until the flavors blend. Remove the bay leaf and serve with mounds of white steamed rice.

1 cup palm or white vinegar

12 cloves garlic, minced

½ teaspoon ground white pepper, or to taste

1 bay leaf

1 tablespoon salt, or to taste

3 tablespoons soy sauce, or to taste

1 pound pork, cut into 1-inch cubes

1 (2-pound) frying chicken, cut into 8 serving-size pieces

3 tablespoons vegetable oil

8 cups cooked rice

Peppered Chicken Adobo

4 TO 6 SERVINGS

Substitute pork for the chicken, or combine the two white meats for entirely different results. Try each of the following Peppered Adobo recipes.

Combine the chicken, soy sauce, vinegar, garlic, peppercorns, bay leaf, and salt with ½ cup water. Stir to coat well, and marinate for 30 minutes. Bring to a boil, lower the heat, cover, and simmer for 10 to 15 minutes. Do not stir. Remove the cover. Stir, and simmer for 7 to 8 minutes, or until the chicken is tender. If desired, add the sherry, and simmer for 1 minute. Remove the bay leaf and peppercorns, and serve hot with fluffy, white rice.

Tip: When adding whole peppercorns a recipe, be sure to remove them before serving, since they are bitter when chewed. Put the peppercorns into a sachet bag made of cheesecloth for easy removal after cooking.

Variations: Use these substitutes for the chicken.

1 (2-pound) spring chicken, cut into 4 to 6 serving-size pieces

½ cup soy sauce, or to taste

⅓ cup palm or apple cider vinegar

12 cloves garlic, minced

8 to 10 black peppercorns

1 bay leaf

½ teaspoon salt, or to taste

⅓ cup cooking sherry, optional

4 to 6 cups cooked white rice

Peppered Chicken Legs and Pork Adobo:
4 chicken legs and ½ pound lean pork, cut into 1-inch cubes.

Peppered Beef Adobo: 1 pound lean beef, cut into 1-inch cubes. Add 1 whole star anise to the marinade (remove before serving).

Peppered Pork Adobo: 2 pounds pork, cut into 1-inch cubes.

Chicken Adobo with Cinnamon and Anise

4 SERVINGS

Mix the chicken, vinegar, soy sauce, tomato, peppercorns, garlic, cinnamon stick, star anise, and bay leaves in a 2-quart pot. Allow the ingredients to marinate for 30 minutes.

Cover and cook for 30 minutes over medium heat. Remove the chicken pieces and place under a broiler for 8 to 10 minutes, or until the chicken is tender and lightly browned.

Continue cooking the marinade until it is reduced by half. Add salt to taste. Remove the cinnamon stick, star anise, and bay leaves, spoon the sauce over the chicken, and serve piping hot.

1 (2-pound) chicken, cut into serving-size pieces

3 tablespoons vinegar

4 tablespoons soy sauce

1 ripe tomato, coarsely chopped

1 teaspoon black peppercorns

4 cloves garlic, minced

1 whole cinnamon stick

1 whole star anise

3 bay leaves

½ teaspoon salt, or to taste

Chicken Adobo in Coconut Milk

4 SERVINGS

Look for patis *and coconut milk in Asian supermarkets.*

Combine the chicken pieces with the vinegar, soy sauce, garlic, ground pepper, bay leaves, peppercorns, and brown sugar in a nonaluminum 4-quart pan. Marinade for 2 to 3 hours in the refrigerator.

Place the pot over high heat and bring to a boil. Lower the heat and simmer for 9 to 10 minutes, or until the chicken is tender. Remove the chicken from the broth and broil for 1 to 2 minutes on each side. Arrange on a heated platter.

Meanwhile, add the *patis* and coconut milk to the sauce and boil until it has reduced by half. Remove the bay leaves. Ladle the sauce over the chicken and serve.

1 (2-pound) chicken, cut into serving-size pieces

1 cup white vinegar

⅓ cup soy sauce

¼ cup minced garlic

½ teaspoon ground black pepper, or to taste

2 bay leaves

½ tablespoon black peppercorns

1 tablespoon raw or brown sugar

1 teaspoon *patis* (fish sauce) or 1 teaspoon salt, or to taste

1 (12-ounce) can coconut milk

Spicy Chicken Adobo

4 TO 6 SERVINGS

In a nonaluminum 4-quart pan, sauté the garlic in the oil for 1 to 2 minutes, or until light brown. Add the chicken, peppercorns, and bay leaves. Sauté for 4 to 5 minutes, or until the chicken is golden brown. Add the soy sauce, vinegar, and ½ cup water. Cover, and simmer for 1½ hours over very low heat, or until the chicken is tender.

4 cloves garlic, minced

3 tablespoons vegetable oil

1 (2-pound) spring chicken, cut into 4 to 6 serving-size pieces

1½ teaspoons black peppercorns, crushed, or to taste

2 bay leaves

¼ cup soy sauce

4 tablespoons palm or white vinegar

Chicken Adobo with Palm Vinegar

4 TO 6 SERVINGS

Try this zesty, marinated chicken stew, flavored with palm vinegar.

Rub the salt and pepper into the chicken pieces. Place in a nonaluminum saucepan with ½ cup water, the bay leaf, garlic, and vinegar. Bring to a boil, then lower the heat, and simmer for 25 to 30 minutes, or until tender. Add more water, if necessary, but allow the juices to be completely absorbed. Remove the bay leaf. Add the oil, and sauté the chicken for 4 to 5 minutes, or until golden brown. Serve steaming hot.

1 teaspoon salt, or to taste

1 teaspoon black peppercorns, crushed

1 (2-pound) spring chicken, cut into 4 to 6 serving-size pieces

1 bay leaf

1 clove garlic, crushed

½ cup palm or white vinegar

¼ cup vegetable oil

Lemon Pepper Chicken Drumsticks Adobo

4 SERVINGS

Rinse the chicken and make slits to the bone. Combine the chicken with the oil, soy sauce, vinegar, garlic, onion, lemon pepper, oregano, and salt in a nonaluminum 4-quart pan. Refrigerate and marinate for 2 to 4 hours, stirring occasionally.

Place the pan over high heat, bring to a boil, then lower the heat, cover, and simmer for 15 to 18 minutes, or until the chicken is tender. Stir occasionally to prevent scorching. Remove the cover and cook for 2 to 3 minutes, or until the liquid is reduced by half. Serve the drumsticks hot with the sauce drizzled over all.

2 pounds chicken drumsticks

2 tablespoons olive oil

½ cup soy sauce

½ cup apple cider vinegar

4 cloves garlic, minced

1 medium onion, minced

1 teaspoon lemon pepper, or to taste

1 teaspoon fresh oregano

1 teaspoon salt, or to taste

Chicken Adobo with Brown Sugar and Cinnamon

4 SERVINGS

Combine all the ingredients in a nonaluminum 4-quart pan. Refrigerate and marinate for 2 to 4 hours, stirring occasionally.

Place the pan over high heat, bring to a boil, then lower the heat, cover, and simmer for 15 to 18 minutes, or until the chicken is tender. Stir occasionally to prevent scorching. Remove the cover and cook for 2 to 3 minutes, or until the liquid is reduced by half.

2 pounds chicken, cut into serving-size pieces

¼ cup soy sauce

6 cloves garlic, minced

1 teaspoon black peppercorns

¼ cup apple cider vinegar

3 bay leaves

1 cinnamon stick

3 tablespoons brown sugar

Chicken Adobo with Coca-Cola

8 SERVINGS

The American influence adds an inimitable twist to the traditional recipe.

Rinse the chicken pieces and pat dry with paper towels. Place half the chicken and 2 tablespoons oil in a large skillet and sauté for 3 minutes each side, or until the chicken is golden brown. Remove from the pan and repeat with the remaining chicken and oil.

Add all the chicken back into the pan. Add the garlic and onion and brown for 2 minutes. Add the vinegar, soy sauce, bay leaves, and potatoes and simmer over medium heat for 7 to 8 minutes. Add the Coca-Cola, reduce the heat, and continue cooking for 8 to 10 minutes, until the chicken is tender and the potatoes are done. Season with the salt and serve.

4 chicken thighs and 4 breasts

4 tablespoons canola oil

6 cloves garlic, minced

I small onion, sliced

⅓ cup apple cider vinegar

⅓ cup soy sauce

2 bay leaves

6 whole new potatoes, unpeeled

½ teaspoon fresh oregano

I cup Coca-Cola

½ teaspoon salt, or to taste

Turkey Adobo

8 SERVINGS

Combine the turkey, soy sauce, vinegar, garlic, peppercorns, and bay leaf in a nonaluminum 4-quart pan. Marinate the turkey for 1 hour or more in the refrigerator. Place the pan over high heat, bring to a boil, then reduce the heat, cover, and simmer, for 20 to 22 minutes, or until tender. Stir occasionally to prevent scorching. Uncover the pan and raise the heat to medium. Continue cooking until the liquid is reduced to half.

2 pounds turkey breast, cut into 2-inch pieces

2 tablespoons soy sauce

⅓ cup red wine vinegar

9 cloves garlic, minced

½ teaspoon cracked black peppercorns

1 bay leaf

Beef Adobo in Coconut Milk

4 TO 6 SERVINGS

Patis *and coconut milk are available in Asian supermarkets.*

Combine the chuck, vinegar, soy sauce, garlic, bay leaves, cracked and whole peppercorns, and sugar in a nonaluminum 4-quart pan. Refrigerate and marinate for 2 to 3 hours.

Place the pan over high heat, bring the mixture to a boil, lower the heat, and simmer for 35 to 40 minutes, or until the beef is tender.

Remove the beef cubes and garlic from the broth. Place in a skillet with the oil, and sauté for 1 to 2 minutes, or until the beef cubes are browned on all sides. Remove the bay leaves from the broth. Return the beef and garlic to the broth. Add the *patis*, and pour in the coconut milk. Bring to a boil, then lower the heat and simmer for 5 to 6 minutes.

3 pounds chuck, cut into 1-inch cubes

¾ cup apple cider vinegar

½ cup soy sauce

9 cloves garlic, minced

4 bay leaves

1 tablespoon cracked black peppercorns

1 tablespoon whole black peppercorns

2 tablespoons raw or brown sugar

¼ cup vegetable oil

1 teaspoon *patis* (fish sauce) or 1 teaspoon salt, or to taste

1 (12-ounce) can coconut milk

Cinnamon-Garlic Beef Adobo

Combine all the ingredients except the rice in a nonaluminum saucepan. Bring to a boil, reduce the heat, and simmer with the cover slightly ajar until the beef is tender and all liquid has evaporated. If the meat is still tough, add ½ cup hot water and continue simmering. When the beef is tender, stir-fry it for 3 to 4 minutes in its own juices, or until it is golden brown. Remove the cinnamon sticks, and serve hot with cooked rice.

2 pounds lean beef, cut in 2-inch pieces

⅓ medium onion, chopped

6 cloves garlic, mashed

½ teaspoon cracked black peppercorns

2 cinnamon sticks

½ cup palm or apple cider vinegar, or enough to cover meat

2 tablespoons soy sauce, or to taste

1 teaspoon salt, or to taste

4 to 6 cups cooked white rice

Onion Garlic Pork Adobo

4 TO 6 SERVINGS

Combine all the ingredients in a heavy saucepan. Bring to a boil, then reduce the heat, and simmer with the cover slightly ajar until the pork is tender and all liquid evaporates. Be sure the pork is thoroughly cooked. If the meat is still tough or pink, add ½ cup hot water and continue simmering. When meat is tender, stir-fry the meat slightly in its own juices until light brown in color. Serve hot, with steamed rice.

2 pounds lean pork, cut in 2-inch pieces

⅓ medium onion, chopped

4 cloves garlic, mashed

½ teaspoon cracked black peppercorns

1 bay leaf, optional

½ cup vinegar, or enough to cover meat

2 tablespoons soy sauce, or to taste

1 teaspoon salt, or to taste

4 to 6 cups cooked white rice

Pork Adobo

BANBEAVE

8 SERVINGS

Filipinos often combine pork with chicken. Experiment with half pork and half boned chicken.

Sauté the pork and garlic in the vegetable oil for 5 to 6 minutes, or until browned. Add the vinegar, bay leaf, peppercorn, salt, soy sauce, sugar, and 1½ cups water. Bring to a boil, and then simmer for 45 to 50 minutes, or until the pork is tender. Serve over hot, fluffy rice.

2 pounds pork, cut into 1-inch cubes

2 cloves garlic, minced

2 tablespoons vegetable oil

¼ cup apple cider vinegar

1 bay leaf

1 whole peppercorn, crushed

½ teaspoon salt, or to taste

1 tablespoon soy sauce, or to taste

1 tablespoon raw or brown sugar

8 cups cooked white rice

VEGETARIAN ADOBO

Spinach Adobo

KANGKONG ADOBO   **4 SERVINGS**

Kangkong is usually available in Asian supermarkets. If not, use spinach or watercress instead.

Thoroughly rinse the *kangkong*. Trim the stems and cut the leaves into 1-inch lengths.

Sauté the garlic in the oil for 1 to 2 minutes in a nonaluminum pan. Add the *kangkong*, vinegar, soy sauce, lime juice, and salt. Stir-fry for 1 to 2 minutes, or just until the leaves wilt. Sprinkle with freshly cracked pepper and serve hot.

2 pounds *kangkong*

6 cloves garlic, minced

¼ cup vegetable oil

¼ cup cider vinegar

3 tablespoons soy sauce

1 tablespoon lime juice

**1 teaspoon salt,
or to taste**

**½ teaspoon cracked
pepper, or to taste**

Eggplant Adobo in Tangy Sauce

4 SERVINGS

When purchasing eggplants, select firm, unblemished vegetables that are heavy for their size. It means they have fewer seeds. Do not store them in plastic; instead, keep them in a paper bag in the refrigerator. If elongated Philippine eggplants are unavailable, substitute the egg-shaped western varieties. Patis is available in Asian supermarkets.

Slice the eggplants into 2-inch cubes. Sauté the eggplant in the oil for 3 to 4 minutes, or until golden brown. Add the soy sauce, vinegar, and garlic to the pan. Simmer over medium heat for 4 to 5 minutes. Fold in the eggplant, and simmer for 5 to 6 minutes, stirring often, or until the eggplant is tender, and the liquid is reduced to half. Add the *patis*. Serve the eggplant hot with the sauce drizzled over all.

2 Philippine eggplants (about 4 cups), cubed

4 tablespoons vegetable oil

4 tablespoons soy sauce

½ cup apple cider vinegar

6 cloves garlic, minced

1 teaspoon *patis* (fish sauce) or ½ teaspoon salt, or to taste

Bamboo Adobo

4 SERVINGS

The tender shoots of the bamboo are a popular Filipino vegetable. Their ivory-colored shoots are conical, usually about 3 inches wide and 4 inches long. Somewhat similar in texture to turnips, they add a subtle flavor to soups, stews, and adobos. If using fresh bamboo shoots, peel, cut them into 1-inch cubes, and parboil for 6 to 8 minutes before adding to the recipe. Bamboo shoots can be purchased at Asian supermarkets whole, sliced, or water-packed in cans.

Sauté the onion and garlic in the oil for 1 to 2 minutes, or until the onion is translucent. Add the pork and shrimp. Stir-fry for 3 to 4 minutes, or until the shrimp is opaque. Add the salt, bouillon, and bamboo shoots. Cover and simmer for 12 to 15 minutes, or until the bamboo shoots are tender. Add the vinegar and pepper. Simmer, uncovered, for 15 to 18 minutes, or until the liquid has been absorbed.

¼ cup minced onion

4 cloves garlic, minced

¼ cup vegetable oil

½ cup coarsely chopped cooked pork

½ cup coarsely chopped shelled shrimp

1 tablespoon salt, or to taste

1 cup vegetable or beef bouillon

3 cups bamboo shoots, cut into 1-inch cubes

¼ cup apple cider vinegar

½ teaspoon freshly ground black pepper, or to taste

Lady's Finger Adobo

Use tender, young okra for best results. Select pods that are 3 to 4 inches long; pods larger than 4 inches are considered mature, are tougher than young okra, and not recommended for use in this recipe. Make sure the okra is dry, firm to the touch, medium to dark green in color, and unblemished with a smooth coating of fuzz.

Rinse and parboil the okra for 5 to 6 minutes. Remove, drain, and transfer to a skillet. Sauté the okra in the oil with the onion and garlic for 4 to 5 minutes, or until the onion is translucent. Stir in the soy sauce, lime juice, and pepper. Simmer for 8 to 9 minutes, or until the okra is tender.

3 cups fresh okra pods

¼ cup vegetable oil

1 cup minced onion

6 cloves garlic, minced

¼ cup soy sauce

¼ cup fresh lime juice

¼ teaspoon ground black pepper, or to taste

Yard-Long Bean Adobo

Yard-long beans really can grow to 3 feet in length, although they are usually picked when about 18 inches long. Related to black-eyed peas, they taste and look like green beans. If long beans are unavailable even in Asian supermarkets, substitute green beans.

Trim and cut the beans into 3-inch lengths (about 3 cups). Using a nonaluminum 4-quart pan, sauté the onion and garlic in the oil for 2 to 3 minutes, or until the onions are translucent. Add the beans, vinegar, soy sauce, bay leaves, and peppercorns. Bring to a boil, then lower the heat, cover, and simmer for 4 to 5 minutes, or until the beans are tender. Add a tablespoon or two of water, if needed, to prevent scorching. Remove the bay leaves and serve hot.

1 bundle yard-long beans

1 medium onion, sliced

3 cloves garlic, minced

3 tablespoons vegetable oil

1/4 cup white vinegar

1/4 cup soy sauce

2 bay leaves

1/2 teaspoon whole black peppercorns

Mussels Adobo

4 SERVINGS

Using a 2-quart pot, bring the mussels, vinegar, garlic, peppercorns, and scant 1 cup water to a boil. Strain the mussels from the broth (reserve the broth). Sauté the mussels in the oil for 1 to 2 minutes, or until tender. Return them to the broth and simmer for 9 to 10 minutes. Add salt to taste.

2 cups shelled mussels

¼ cup white vinegar

6 cloves garlic, minced

½ teaspoon whole black peppercorns

2 tablespoons vegetable oil

½ teaspoon ground rock salt, or to taste

Sea Bass Adobo

4 SERVINGS

The vinegar, ginger, and jalapeño combination gives this dish its piquant flavor. Experiment with porgy, mullet, or bluefish for variety.

If patis *is unavailable, look in Asian supermarkets or substitute 1 teaspoon rock salt or 2 tablespoons soy sauce, and add 2 teaspoons freshly squeezed lemon juice.*

To a 3-quart nonaluminum pot, add the vinegar, ginger, garlic, pepper, patis, and ½ cup water. Bring to a rolling boil for 2 to 3 minutes.

Add the fish and oil, lower heat, cover, and simmer for 8 to 9 minutes, or until the fish is done and flakes easily. Carefully lift out the fish with wide utensils, such as spatulas or flat strainers, to keep the fish whole. Transfer to a heated platter. Top with mounds of tiny green onion rings and serve steaming hot.

½ cup palm or white vinegar

3 tablespoons julienned ginger

2 tablespoons minced garlic

I jalapeño pepper, coarsely chopped

I teaspoon *patis* (fish sauce)

I pound sea bass, cleaned but left whole

I tablespoon olive oil

I cup finely sliced green onions

Catfish Adobo

4 SERVINGS

Marinate the catfish in the vinegar, ginger, garlic, and pepper overnight, or at least for 4 hours.

Strain the ginger and garlic bits from the marinade. Add the bits to a nonaluminum Dutch oven or 4-quart pot, and sauté in the oil for 1 to 2 minutes, or until golden brown. Add the catfish and marinade. Bring to a boil, and then lower the heat. Turning the fish several times, simmer for 9 to 10 minutes, or until it is done and flakes easily.

2 pounds catfish

I cup white vinegar

2 tablespoons minced fresh ginger

2 tablespoons minced garlic

½ teaspoon ground white pepper, or to taste

¼ cup vegetable oil

Squid Adobo

4 SERVINGS

Rinse and clean the squid, being careful to remove the cuttle and ink sack. Place the squid in a nonaluminum pot with the vinegar, soy sauce, garlic, pepper, and 1 cup water. Simmer over low heat for 8 to 9 minutes, or until the squid is just done and tender. Be careful not to overcook; the squid becomes tough or rubbery. Remove the squid and strain the garlic from the broth, reserving the liquid.

Heat the oil in a nonaluminum pan. Add the cooked garlic, onion, and tomatoes. Sauté for 2 to 3 minutes, or until the onion is translucent and the tomatoes are soft. Add the squid to the vegetable mixture, spooning the vegetables over all. Simmer over low heat for 3 to 4 four minutes. Blend in the broth and bring to a boil. Serve steaming hot.

I medium (1-pound) squid

½ cup apple cider vinegar

4 tablespoons soy sauce

9 cloves garlic, minced

½ teaspoon freshly ground black pepper, or to taste

2 tablespoons vegetable oil

⅓ cup coarsely chopped onion

2 cups coarsely chopped and drained plum tomatoes

Clam Adobo

4 SERVINGS

If patis is unavailable, look in Asian supermarkets or substitute $1/2$ teaspoon rock salt or 1 tablespoon soy sauce, and add 1 teaspoon freshly squeezed lemon juice.

Using a 2-quart pot, bring the clams, vinegar, garlic, peppercorns, and scant 1 cup water to a boil. Strain the clams from the broth. Sauté the clams in the oil for 1 to 2 minutes, or until tender. Return them to the broth and simmer for 9 to 10 minutes. Add the *patis* and serve steaming hot.

2 cups shelled clams

$1/4$ cup white vinegar

6 cloves garlic, minced

$1/2$ teaspoon whole black peppercorns

2 tablespoons vegetable oil

$1/2$ teaspoon *patis* (fish sauce)

Trout Adobo

4 SERVINGS

For variety, try bluefish.

Clean and rinse the trout. Combine the vinegar, bay leaves, salt, garlic, pepper, and ¼ cup water in a nonaluminum 4-quart pan. Add the trout, and marinate for 1 hour.

Bring to a rolling boil. Lower the heat, cover, and simmer for 5 to 6 minutes. Remove the trout and drain. Bring the broth to a boil and cook until it is reduced by half. Remove the bay leaves.

Meanwhile, sauté the trout in a skillet with the oil for 3 to 4 minutes, or until golden brown. Ladle the sauce over the fish. Simmer for 2 to 3 minutes, or until the fish is done and flakes easily.

2 pounds trout

¼ cup white vinegar

2 bay leaves

½ tablespoon salt, or to taste

6 cloves garlic, minced

½ teaspoon ground white pepper, or to taste

¼ cup vegetable oil

Shrimp Adobo in Coconut Milk

4 SERVINGS

Coconut milk is available in Asian supermarkets and some grocery stores.

Combine the vinegar, garlic, salt, pepper, shrimp, and ¼ cup water in a nonaluminum 4-quart pan. Marinate for 1 hour.

Place pan over high heat and bring to a boil, uncovered. Stirring often, boil the shrimp for 8 to 10 minutes, or until the liquid has nearly evaporated. Pour in the coconut milk and simmer for 10 minutes, or until the sauce has thickened. Serve piping hot in individual bowls with the sauce.

1 cup white vinegar

9 cloves garlic, minced

1 teaspoon salt, or to taste

¼ teaspoon ground white pepper, or to taste

2 pounds large or jumbo fresh shrimp, cleaned but unshelled

2 (12-ounce) cans coconut milk

SOUPS

In the Philippines, food is not served in sequential courses. It is served all at once like a buffet. A variety of textures is the goal for each meal: smooth, crunchy, soft, and chewy taste sensations. Rice, of course, is the basis for all meals. With this, broiled, fried, stewed, or roasted, meat, fish, or poultry give the meal crunchy and chewy textures. Lumpias (Filipino egg rolls) incorporate a crispy texture. A cup of soup, such as *sinigang*, lends a smooth texture to the meal.

Whitefish Chowder with Watercress

4 SERVINGS

Traditionally this chowder is prepared with talbos ng ampalaya, *a leafy green vegetable common to the Philippines, but watercress or spinach is an excellent substitute.*

In a 2-quart saucepan, combine the tomatoes, green peppers, onion, and salt with 3 cups water; bring to a boil. Add the fish and simmer for 5 to 8 minutes, or until the fish is tender. Reserving 4 sprigs for the garnish, add the watercress, and heat for 1 minute. Ladle into preheated bowls, garnish with the sprigs, and serve at once.

2 medium plum tomatoes, cut into 1/2-inch pieces

2 medium green peppers, cut into 1/4-inch pieces

1 small (1/2 cup) coarsely chopped onion

1 1/2 teaspoons salt

1 pound whitefish, boned and cut into 1/2-inch pieces

1/3 cup chopped fresh watercress

Lapu-Lapu Tinola

4 TO 6 SERVINGS

Add the tender, young leaves of dahon ng sili, *chili peppers, available in Asian supermarkets, to the* tinola *during the last few minutes of cooking. The leaves exude a mildly piquant flavor, not quite as spicy as that of its fruit, chili peppers.*

Rinse the fish, remove any bones, and slice into 1-inch chunks. Place in a 4-quart pot and add 10 cups water, ginger, and tomatoes. Cover, bring to a boil, then lower the heat and simmer for 5 to 6 minutes, stirring occasionally. Add the peppers, green onions (reserving 2 tablespoons for garnish), salt, pepper, and spinach. Simmer for 4 to 5 minutes, or until the fish flakes easily and the vegetables are tender-crisp. Ladle into preheated bowls. Garnish with a sprinkling of green pepper rings. Serve with hot steamed rice.

2 pounds fresh lapu-lapu fish, dressed

2 tablespoons minced fresh ginger

4 ripe plum tomatoes, diced

6 banana peppers, or 2 medium green peppers, diced

6 green onions, thinly sliced

1 tablespoon salt, or to taste

1/2 teaspoon ground black pepper, or to taste

1 cup spinach or *dahon ng sili* (chili pepper leaves)

4 to 6 cups steamed rice

Chicken Tinola with Green Papaya

4 TO 6 SERVINGS

Patis *and* dahon ng sili *are available in Asian supermarkets.*

Using a wok or Dutch oven, sauté the garlic, onion, and ginger in the oil for 1 to 2 minutes, or until the onion is translucent. Add the chicken and sauté for 8 to 10 minutes, or until browned. Add the *patis* and 4 cups water. Bring to a boil. Lower the heat, cover, and simmer for 30 to 35 minutes, or until the chicken is tender.

Add the papaya and simmer for 5 minutes, or until tender. Add the salt, pepper, and spinach. Cover and simmer for 2 to 3 minutes, or until the leaves are wilted. Serve hot.

3 cloves garlic, minced

1 small onion, finely chopped

2 tablespoons chopped ginger

2 tablespoons vegetable oil

1 (3-pound) chicken, cut into serving-size pieces

2 tablespoons *patis* (fish sauce)

1 green papaya, peeled and cubed

1 tablespoon salt, or to taste

1/2 teaspoon ground black pepper, or to taste

1 1/2 cups spinach or *dahon ng sili* (chili pepper leaves)

Mung Bean Soup with Shrimp

GINISANG MONGO   **4 TO 6 SERVINGS**

Soak the beans overnight (very important). Be sure the water covers the beans completely. The following morning, rub the beans together to easily remove any remaining hulls. Rinse the beans, drain, and set aside.

Using a 6-quart pot, add the oil, onion, and garlic. Sauté for 1 to 2 minutes over medium heat, or until the onions are translucent. Add the drained beans, broth, and ginger. Bring to a boil, lower the heat, cover, and simmer for 35 to 40 minutes, or until the beans are tender and the soup has thickened.

Add the salt and pepper, along with the cooked shrimp. Simmer for 2 to 3 minutes, or until the shrimp are heated through. Serve hot, ladled into prewarmed bowls.

Tip: Use diced, cooked pork instead of shrimp for an entirely different soup.

2 cups dry *mongo* beans (mung beans), hulled

2 tablespoons vegetable oil

1 medium yellow onion, thinly sliced

2 cloves garlic, minced

5 cups chicken or vegetable broth

1 tablespoon minced fresh ginger

½ tablespoon salt, or to taste

½ teaspoon ground black pepper, or to taste

1 pound shrimp, shelled, cleaned, and cooked

Garlic Soup

This aromatic soup is used as both a fiesta dish and sore-throat remedy.

Brown the croutons in 1 tablespoon oil in a wok or 2-quart saucepan for 1 minute. Set aside.

Heat the remaining 2 tablespoons oil, and sauté the garlic and onion for 1 to 2 minutes, or until the onion is translucent. Add the broth, salt, and pepper. Bring to boil, reduce the heat, cover, and simmer for 5 to 7 minutes, or until the broth is steaming.

Divide the croutons, potatoes, and chicken among four preheated soup bowls. Ladle the broth over all, and serve immediately.

1 cup stale bread cubes

3 tablespoons olive oil

3 cloves garlic, minced

2 tablespoons minced onion

3½ cups vegetable broth

½ teaspoon salt, or to taste

¼ teaspoon ground black pepper, or to taste

1 cup diced boiled potatoes

1 cup diced chicken, ham, or firm tofu

Chicken Soup with Sotanghon

6 SERVINGS

Sotanghon *are transparent bean noodles, also known as cellophane noodles. Try this Filipino-style chicken and noodle soup. Look for* tainga sa daga, patis, *and* sotanghon *in Asian supermarkets.*

Add the chicken and 10 cups water to a 4-quart pot. Bring to a boil, lower the heat, cover, and simmer for 18 to 20 minutes, or until the chicken is tender. When cool enough to handle, remove the chicken, reserving the broth. Bone and dice the chicken.

Using a wok or skillet, sauté the garlic, onion, and chicken in the oil for 1 to 2 minutes. Add the mushrooms to the skillet and sauté for 3 to 4 minutes, or until the chicken is lightly browned, and the vegetables are tender-crisp.

Return the chicken-vegetable mixture to the broth. Add *patis* and pepper, and simmer for 15 to 18 minutes.

Meanwhile, soak the *sotanghon* in hot water for 1 minute to soften. Cut the noodles into 2-inch lengths. Add the *sotanghon* to the broth during the last minute of cooking, and simmer for 1 minute. Ladle the soup into preheated bowls. Garnish with green onions and serve steaming hot.

I chicken, cut into serving-size pieces

3 cloves garlic, minced

I medium onion, diced

3 tablespoons olive oil

½ pound *tainga sa daga* (native mushrooms) or shiitake mushrooms, sliced

I tablespoon *patis* (fish sauce) or I teaspoon salt, or to taste

½ teaspoon ground black pepper

8 ounces *sotanghon*

3 green onions, thinly sliced

Chicken Rice Soup with Ginger

ARROZ CALDO CON POLLO   4 SERVINGS

Make this comfort food a day ahead to allow the flavors to marry. Besides being traditional Christmas Eve fare, the soup is also a cold remedy.

Using a 3-quart pot, sauté 2 tablespoons garlic, the ginger, and onion in 2 tablespoons oil for 3 to 4 minutes, or until the garlic is golden, and the onion is translucent. Add the rice and stir-fry for 2 to 3 minutes. Slowly add 10 cups water to the rice mixture. Bring the soup to a boil, stirring occasionally. Lower the heat, add the chicken, and simmer for 30 to 35 minutes, or until the rice is tender. Add the salt during the final 5 minutes of cooking.

Meanwhile, sauté the remaining garlic in the remaining 2 tablespoons oil until the garlic is a golden brown.

Serve the soup in a preheated tureen. Garnish with the sautéed garlic, green onion rings, and black pepper.

Note: *Patis* is a fish sauce used for seasoning nearly every Filipino dish: chicken, beef, pork, fish, shrimp, crabs, and other seafood. However, *patis* is an acquired taste. A good substitute is rock or iodized salt. Other substitutes for *patis* are a mixture of soy sauce and freshly squeezed lemon juice or soy sauce and kumquats. *Patis* is available in Asian supermarkets.

Ingredients

- ½ cup minced garlic
- 1 (2-inch) piece ginger, coarsely chopped or squeezed through a garlic press
- 1 large onion, peeled and coarsely chopped
- ¼ cup vegetable oil
- 1½ cups uncooked rice
- 1 (2-pound) chicken, cut into serving-size pieces
- 1½ teaspoons salt or *patis* (fish sauce)
- ½ cup finely sliced green onions
- ½ teaspoon ground black pepper, or to taste

Philippine Wonton Soup

Combine the pork, shrimp, water chestnuts, and eggs with half of the green onions. Blend in the salt and pepper and mix well. Place 1 teaspoon of the filling on the center of each wrapper. Moisten the edges, fold in a triangle, and bring the two lateral corners together.

The stuffed wontons can be frozen at this point. Freeze in a single layer on a baking sheet, and then transfer to resealable plastic bags. (Thaw before cooking.)

Bring the chicken stock to a rolling boil. Carefully lower the stuffed wonton wrappers into the stock, and simmer for 20 to 21 minutes, or until the pork is thoroughly cooked and no longer pink. Add the pea pods to the stock, and simmer for 4 to 5 minutes, or until tender-crisp. Serve steaming hot, garnished with the remaining green onions.

½ pound ground pork

½ pound shrimp, shelled, deveined, and chopped

½ cup water chestnuts, drained and chopped

2 eggs

6 green onions, finely sliced

1 teaspoon salt, or to taste

¼ teaspoon ground black pepper, or to taste

20 wonton wrappers (see Wrapper Triangles recipe page 108)

2 quarts chicken stock

½ pound fresh pea pods, trimmed

Creamy Corn Soup

4 SERVINGS

Heat the oil in a wok or 2-quart saucepan, and sauté the onions and garlic for 1 to 2 minutes, or until the onions are translucent. Add the corn, broth, and milk to the onion mixture. Bring just to a boil, reduce heat, cover, and simmer for 10 to 12 minutes. Season with salt and pepper. Serve hot.

Tip: For more texture, add an additional ½ cup fresh corn, cut from the cob.

1 tablespoon vegetable oil

¼ cup minced onions

1 clove garlic, minced

1 cup fresh or frozen corn, chopped to a paste

2½ cups vegetable broth

1 cup soy milk

½ teaspoon salt, or to taste

¼ teaspoon ground white pepper, or to taste

RICE

Rice forms a large part of the Filipino diet. It is eaten with all meals, including breakfast. In the morning, rice left over from the previous evening's meal is fried with sausages. At lunch, steamed rice is served with assorted vegetables, meats, and fish. For mid-afternoon snacks, known as *merienda cena*, sweet rice cakes are featured, and, at dinner, rice forms the basis of an endless variety of dishes.

Rice can be cooked in broth, seasoned with yellow saffron, or sautéed with plum tomatoes. It takes on the color and flavor of the ingredients with which it is prepared. Because rice is such a ubiquitous part of Filipino cuisine, it is served as a backdrop to the meal, the proverbial straight man to the stand-up comic, the subtle foil complementing the rich meal.

Rice is the blank canvas for each picture-perfect meal. Salty, sour, and spicy flavors are especially savory when eaten against the mild counterpoint of rice. Today traditional varieties of rice have been replaced with new ones. Check Asian markets for gourmet rices, such as *Calrose*, a short-grain, sticky white rice, *malagkit* (glutinous rice), *pinipig* (green rice), and *pirurutong* (purple glutinous rice).

Steamed Rice

An electric rice cooker makes quick work of steamed rice, but, to make rice the traditional way, use a heavy steel pot.

Rinse rice well and drain. Combine the rice and salt with 4 cups water. Bring to a boil, then lower the heat, cover, and simmer for 13 to 15 minutes, or until the water has been absorbed, and the rice is tender.

2 cups white rice

I teaspoon salt, or to taste

Filipino Fried Rice

4 SERVINGS

Fried rice is a favorite Filipino dish for using leftovers: shellfish, ham, beef, pork, chicken, or nearly any vegetable. Use day-old rice and mince ½ cup leftover meat, fish, or vegetables to create a different side dish every time!

Add 1 tablespoon oil and the eggs to a skillet. Stir-fry the eggs and chop coarsely. Remove from skillet and place on paper towels.

Sauté the onion and green peppers in the remaining 1 tablespoon oil for 3 to 4 minutes, or until the vegetables are tender. Fold in the cooked rice. Gradually add the eggs and shrimp, stirring all the while. Season with the soy sauce and pepper. Cover and allow to simmer for 4 to 5 minutes, or until the flavors have married.

2 tablespoons vegetable oil

3 eggs, lightly beaten

I medium onion, minced

I large green pepper, minced

4 cups cooked rice

½ cup cooked shrimp, minced

I teaspoon soy sauce, or to taste

¼ teaspoon ground black pepper, or to taste

Fast Philippine Fried Rice

No meal is complete without rice, breakfast included. For a quick morning meal, whip up this easy version of fried rice, and serve with sausages and eggs.

Using a wok or large skillet, sauté the garlic in the oil for 1 to 2 minutes, or until lightly browned. Add ½ cup water and the remaining ingredients. Stir-fry over medium heat for 7 to 8 minutes, or until the mixture is heated evenly. Be careful not to scorch. Add another tablespoon water, if necessary. Serve steaming hot.

4 cloves garlic, minced

¼ cup vegetable oil

¼ cup minced shallots

4 cups cooked rice

1 tablespoon soy sauce

1 teaspoon salt, or to taste

¼ teaspoon ground black pepper, or to taste

EGGS

Eggs are a principal source of protein in the Philippines. *Itlog-na-maalat*, salted chicken or duck eggs, are dyed red or purple, then chopped and mixed with vegetables. Duck eggs are believed to be superior for making pastries and noodles. *Balut*, a fertilized duck egg, is a nutritious delicacy that is believed to be aphrodisiacal.

Wonton Baskets

Preheat the oven to 375° F. Brush the wonton wrapper with 4 tablespoons melted butter. Place 2 wonton wrappers at angles in each section of a muffin pan. Bake for 7 to 9 minutes, or until golden brown. Remove and set aside.

Scramble the beaten eggs in a skillet with the remaining 4 tablespoons butter, ham, parsley, milk, and salt. Spoon the mixture into the wonton baskets and sprinkle with grated cheese. Place in the oven for 2 to 3 minutes, or until the cheese melts.

24 wonton wrappers
(see recipe page 108)

8 tablespoons butter

5 eggs, lightly beaten

½ cup finely chopped ham

1 tablespoon minced
fresh parsley

1 tablespoon milk

¼ teaspoon salt,
or to taste

¼ cup grated cheddar
cheese

Chick'n Eggs

If using fresh quail eggs, place eggs in a pan, barely cover with cold water, bring to a boil, and simmer for 4 minutes. Cool eggs and remove shells. If using jarred quail eggs, rinse and pat dry.

Combine the chicken, parsley, green onion, mustard, salt, 1 cup bread crumbs, and 1 beaten egg in a bowl. Dip the quail eggs into the remaining beaten egg. Press 2 tablespoons of the chicken mixture around each quail egg to form a small ball. Dip each quail egg ball first in the flour, again in the beaten egg, and then roll in the remaining 1 cup bread crumbs.

Using a wok or 2-quart saucepan, deep-fry the eggs in hot oil for 1 to 2 minutes, or until well browned. Remove and drain on paper towels. Cut the quail egg balls in half. Serve "sunny-side" up, with the quail egg set in the middle of the "nest." Serve with chili sauce or salsa, if desired.

12 fresh or jarred quail eggs

1 cup finely chopped cooked chicken

1 tablespoon chopped fresh parsley

1 tablespoon chopped green onion

2 teaspoons prepared mustard

$\frac{1}{2}$ teaspoon salt, or to taste

2 cups dry bread crumbs

2 eggs, lightly beaten

1 tablespoon flour

2 cups vegetable oil

$\frac{1}{2}$ cup chili sauce or salsa, optional

Salted Eggs

ITLOG NA MAALAT   YIELDS I DOZEN

Salted eggs are popular as breakfast fare and side dishes. Just slice the eggs and serve interspersed with sliced plum tomatoes.

Place the eggs in a ceramic or plastic container. Cover the eggs with water and add enough salt to create a super-saturated solution. Continue adding salt to the water until the salt no longer dissolves. Cover and refrigerate for 2 weeks. Remove the eggs from the saltwater.

12 eggs

2 cups salt, or as needed

6 drops red food coloring, optional

To hard-boil eggs, place eggs in a saucepan and cover with cold water. Bring to a boil, then reduce the heat just to the boiling point, cover, and simmer for 15 to 18 minutes. Remove from heat and cover with cold water until cool.

Traditionally the eggs are colored red to distinguish them from ordinary eggs. To dye the eggs, add the food coloring to hot water. Dip the eggs into the red solution for 1 to 2 minutes, or until they reach the desired color. Refrigerate until ready to use. Serve chilled and sliced.

PANCIT

Pancit is the general Filipino term for noodles. The etymology of *pancit* is Chinese, as is the origin of noodles. Even the imagery of noodles is Chinese, symbolizing good fortune, prosperity, and longevity. The longer the noodles, the longer the life, which is why extraordinarily long noodles are often served on birthdays.

Many varieties of Filipino noodles are available: *bihon* (rice stick noodles), *canton* (Chinese wheat noodles), *mami* (wide Chinese egg noodles), *miki* (flat egg noodles), *misua* or *miswa* (angel hair pasta), *sotanghon* (transparent bean or cellophane noodles), and *udon* (wide Japanese noodles).

Each type of noodle has a different texture and, because of this, a different taste as it absorbs the flavors of the ingredients with which it is prepared. *Pancit* is easy to prepare. Simply take care not to overcook the noodles.

Pork Chop Noodles

4 SERVINGS

Simmer the pork chops in the broth for 20 minutes, or until thoroughly cooked and tender. Remove from the liquid and drain, reserving the broth. When cool, cut the meat from the bone and slice into ¼-inch strips.

Using a wok or heavy skillet, stir-fry the olive oil, garlic, and brussels sprouts for 3 to 4 minutes. Add the celery and onion. Stir-fry for 5 minutes, or until the vegetables are tender. Add the soy sauce. Stir in the pork slices. Stir-fry for 3 to 4 minutes, or until the flavors have blended. Serve over hot noodles.

4 lean pork chops

2 cups beef or vegetable broth

2 tablespoons olive oil

4 cloves garlic, minced

1 pound brussels sprouts, halved

4 stalks celery, cut into 1-inch pieces

1 large onion, cut into 1-inch pieces

1 tablespoon soy sauce, or to taste

Rice Noodles

4 SERVINGS

Bihon *are available in Asian supermarkets.*

Combine the reserved broth with water to equal 2 quarts. Bring to a boil. Add the noodles. Salt to taste, bring to a boil again, and cook for 2 to 3 minutes, or until the rice noodles are tender. Drain and serve.

1 (14-ounce) package *bihon* **(rice-stick noodles)**

1 teaspoon salt, or to taste

Noodles Cantonese-Style

Patis *is available in Asian supermarkets.*

Sauté the garlic and onion in 2 tablespoons vegetable oil until the garlic is golden brown and the onion is translucent. Add another 2 tablespoons oil, and sauté the shrimp, sausage, pork, and chicken until the shrimp is pink. Reserve 1 cup for garnish.

Add the shrimp juice or chicken broth to the meat mixture. Simmer for 4 to 5 minutes. Add the soy sauce, optional *patis*, and fresh peas.

Blanch the cabbage wedges and julienned carrots in boiling water for 1 minute. Remove, drain, and add to the meat mixture. Fold in the cooked noodles. Simmer for 5 minutes, stirring constantly to blend the flavors.

Season with the sesame oil, salt, and pepper. Transfer to a heated platter. Garnish with the reserved sautéed meats, green onion slices, and lemon wedges.

*Tip: To make shrimp juice, steep the shrimp shells in 1 cup water. Strain the shrimp juice.

5 cloves garlic, minced

1 large onion, peeled and coarsely chopped

1/2 cup vegetable oil

1/2 cup raw shrimp, peeled and deveined

1/2 cup thinly sliced Chinese sausage or pepperoni

1/2 cup diced boiled pork

1/2 cup boned and flaked boiled chicken

1 cup shrimp juice* or chicken broth

2 tablespoons soy sauce

1 tablespoon *patis* (fish sauce), optional

1/2 cup fresh green peas

1/2 small cabbage, cut into 4 wedges

2 carrots, peeled and julienned

4 cups cooked noodles

2 tablespoons sesame oil, or to taste

1 teaspoon salt, or to taste

1/2 teaspoon pepper, or to taste

1/2 cup green onions, thinly sliced for garnish

1 lemon

PANCIT

Chicken Noodles with Bok Choy

Simmer the chicken in the broth for 12 to 15 minutes, or until tender. Remove from the liquid and drain, reserving the broth. When cool, bone the chicken and slice it into ¼-inch strips.

Using a wok or heavy skillet, stir-fry the olive oil, garlic, and bok choy for 1 to 2 minutes. Add the celery and onion. Stir-fry for 5 minutes, or until the vegetables are tender. Add the soy sauce. Stir in the chicken. Stir-fry for 3 to 4 minutes, or until the flavors have blended. Serve over hot rice noodles (see recipe page 98).

**4 pieces chicken
(breasts or legs)**

2 cups chicken broth

2 tablespoons olive oil

4 cloves garlic, minced

**1 pound bok choy,
coarsely chopped**

**4 stalks celery,
cut into 1-inch pieces**

**1 large onion,
cut into 1-inch pieces**

**1 tablespoon soy sauce,
or to taste**

Tiger Prawn Noodles

Peel the prawns or shrimp, leaving the tails on. Devein, rinse, and pat dry. Dip in egg white. Coat with 1 tablespoon cornstarch and set aside. Bone and slice the chicken breast into 1-inch strips. Dip in egg white. Coat with 1 tablespoon cornstarch.

Sauté the garlic, onion, pork, and chicken liver for 1 minute in the olive oil, stirring constantly. Add the prawns and chicken meat. Sauté for 3 to 4 minutes. Season with the salt and soy sauce. Pour in the broth and bring to a boil. Add the carrot, cauliflower, cabbage, pea pods, and *kutsay*, and cook for 2 to 3 minutes, stirring constantly. Dissolve the remaining 1 tablespoon cornstarch in 2 tablespoons cold water. Add the cornstarch to the broth, and stir for 1 to 2 minutes, or until the mixture has thickened. Add the noodles and cook 3 minutes. Serve hot.

1 pound tiger prawns or shrimp

1 egg white, lightly beaten

3 tablespoons cornstarch

1 chicken breast

2 cloves garlic, minced

1 medium onion, chopped

2 ounces lean pork, coarsely chopped

4 chicken livers, coarsely chopped (optional)

3 tablespoons olive oil

1 teaspoon salt, or to taste

1 tablespoon soy sauce, or to taste

1 1/2 cups broth

1 carrot, peeled and julienned

1 head cauliflower, cut into florets

4 cabbage leaves, shredded

1/4 pound pea pods, trimmed

1/3 cup *kutsay* (leeks)

1 (14-ounce) package *pancit* (rice noodles)

Pork Steak with Asparagus and Noodles

8 SERVINGS

Feel free to substitute the vegetables with what is either in season or on hand.

Using a large wok, sauté the pork, onion, and garlic in the soy sauce and vegetable oil for 8 to 10 minutes, or until the pork is browned and thoroughly cooked. Add the vegetables in the order in which it takes the longest to cook. For example, first add the celery and carrots. Stir-fry for 3 minutes. Next add the broccoli, asparagus, and pea pods. Stir-fry for 3 minutes. Add the mushrooms, peppers, and zucchini, and stir-fry for 4 minutes, or until all the vegetables are crisp-tender. Be careful not to overcook.

3 pounds pork steaks, cut in ½ -inch strips, all fat trimmed

1 large onion, diced

2 cloves garlic, minced

3 tablespoons soy sauce, or to taste

4 tablespoons vegetable oil

1 cup coarsely chopped celery

4 medium carrots, thinly sliced

½ pound broccoli florets, cut into bite-size pieces

½ pound asparagus, tough, white ends removed, cut into bite-size pieces

½ pound pea pods, trimmed

¼ pound mushrooms, sliced

1 red bell pepper, julienned

1 green bell pepper, julienned

While vegetables are cooking, gradually add the ginger, curry powder, cloves, and allspice. Dissolve the cornstarch in 2 tablespoons cold water and whisk into the mixture to thicken. Cook the Ramen noodles according to package directions. Drain and add the seasoning packets. During the last 5 minutes of cooking, fold the noodles into the vegetable mixture, stirring gently. Simmer for 5 minutes, or until the vegetables are tender. Remove from the heat and let stand for 5 minutes for the flavors to blend. Serve in a preheated tureen.

1 yellow bell pepper, julienned

1 medium zucchini, cut into 1/8-inch slices

1/2 teaspoon ground ginger

1 teaspoon curry powder

1/4 teaspoon ground cloves

1/4 teaspoon ground allspice

2 teaspoon cornstarch

4 packages pork-flavored Ramen noodles, with seasoning packets

Venison with Noodles

6 SERVINGS

Wild game is still common on many of the Philippine islands. However, if venison is unavailable, other wild game, beef, or pork may be substituted. Look for sotanghon in Asian supermarkets.

Using a 2-quart pot, brown the meat in the oil, and remove. To the drippings, add the garlic, onions, and green peppers. Stir-fry for 3 to 4 minutes, or until the onions are translucent. Return the meat to the pot. Add the diced carrots, salt, soy sauce, and 4 cups water. Bring to a boil, then lower the heat and simmer for 20 to 25 minutes.

Stir in the mushrooms and cabbage and simmer for 5 to 7 minutes, or until the meat and vegetables are tender. Add the *sotanghon*. Simmer for 1 to 2 minutes, or until the noodles are elastic. Do not overcook.

1 pound venison,
cut into ½-inch pieces

2 tablespoons
vegetable oil

3 cloves garlic, minced

2 medium onions, minced

2 medium green peppers,
coarsely chopped

2 carrots, diced

1 teaspoon salt, or to
taste

1 tablespoon soy sauce,
or to taste

¼ pound mushrooms,
sliced

2 cups shredded cabbage

1 (14-ounce) package
sotanghon
(bean thread noodles)

Angel Hair Pancit

4 SERVINGS

Using a large skillet, sauté the onion and garlic in the oil for 1 to 2 minutes, or until onions are translucent. Add the green beans, carrots, celery, mushrooms, and chicken. Stir-fry until the vegetables are tender-crisp and the chicken is thoroughly cooked. Blend in the soy sauce. Fold the mixture into the angel hair pasta. Garnish with sliced eggs and serve steaming hot.

1 medium onion, diced

1 clove garlic, minced

2 tablespoon vegetable oil

1 cup green beans, cut diagonally

2 carrots, pared and julienned

2 stalks celery, finely chopped

1 cup coarsely chopped mushrooms

1 cup skinned and diced chicken

¼ cup soy sauce, or to taste

1 (7-ounce) package angel hair pasta, cooked and drained

3 hard-boiled eggs, sliced

Shrimp, Chicken, and Pork Pancit

8 SERVINGS

Try this triple-treat, one-pan meal when you want a sumptuous dinner—in 30 minutes. Pancit bihon *are available at Asian supermarkets.*

Pour the oil into a preheated wok or large skillet over high heat, swirling to coat all sides of the pan. Sauté the garlic just as the oil begins to smoke. Quickly stir in the onion, shrimp, chicken, and pork. Stir-fry for 4 to 5 minutes. Add the salt, pepper, water chestnuts, snow peas, and cabbage. Stir-fry for 1 to 2 minutes, or until the vegetables are tender-crisp, and the chicken and shrimp are done.

Unwrap the rice noodles. Soak in hot water from the tap, for 2 to 3 minutes. Drain and set aside.

Add the soy sauce and noodles to the vegetables. Toss to mix thoroughly. Transfer to a warmed platter. Serve immediately, garnished with green onions.

2 tablespoons vegetable oil

2 cloves garlic, minced

1 medium onion, thinly sliced

8 medium shrimp, shelled and deveined

1 cup thinly sliced chicken

1 cup thinly sliced roast pork

1 teaspoon salt, or to taste

½ teaspoon ground white pepper, or to taste

¼ cup thinly sliced water chestnuts

½ cup julienned snow peas

1 cup shredded cabbage

1 pound rice noodles (*pancit bihon*)

3 tablespoons soy sauce

2 green onions, finely chopped

LUMPIA

Lumpia is the Filipino version of Chinese egg rolls. Their popularity is due to their scrumptious taste, endless variety, and easy preparation. Ingredient substitution is not only encouraged, it is practically mandatory. Because of this, lumpia is a perfect way to use leftover meat, fish, chicken, tofu, or vegetables. Lumpia wrappers are available in Asian supermarkets.

Filipinos each have their own way of sealing the lumpia wrappers. Most use a drop of water. Some prefer using lightly beaten egg white. Still others make a paste of 1 tablespoon cornstarch mixed with 1 tablespoon cold water. Whichever method you use, dip your finger in it and lightly smear the inside edge of the wrapper. Press to seal.

Round Wrappers

Combine the flour and egg with 1 cup water. Whisk until smooth. Lightly oil a nonstick skillet or crepe pan. Spoon or brush 1 tablespoon of the mixture onto the pan. When the dough is a pale brown and begins to pull away from the sides of the pan, carefully lift the wrapper off and set aside. Repeat until the batter is gone. Wrappers may be made ahead and frozen.

1 cup flour

1 egg, lightly beaten

1 teaspoon vegetable oil

Wrapper Triangles

Sift the flour and salt. One at a time, knead in the egg yolks, gradually adding ¼ cup water. Knead until the dough is smooth and elastic. Roll out on a lightly floured board until paper-thin. Slice into triangles, the sides measuring 3 inches. They can last up to a week tightly covered with plastic wrap and refrigerated.

2 cups flour

¼ teaspoon salt

3 egg yolks, lightly beaten

Mix-Match Lumpia

YIELDS 20

Try mix-matching the following ingredients to create your own lumpia.

½ cup vegetable oil

I pound meat or other protein:

Cubed tofu

Chopped beef

Minced pork

Chopped, shelled shrimp or any shellfish

Chopped, boned fish of any sort

Flaked cooked tuna

Chopped chicken

Chopped turkey

Minced ham

½ cup minced onions

¼ cup of any 2 or 3 vegetables:

Chopped water chestnuts

Chopped bamboo shoots

Chopped mushrooms

Chopped green beans

Chopped sweet green or red peppers

Chopped cabbage or bok choy

Chopped carrots

Chopped jicama

Chopped celery

Chopped bean sprouts

Diced, par-boiled potatoes

Diced, par-boiled sweet potatoes

Finely sliced green onion

I teaspoon salt, or to taste

½ teaspoon ground black pepper, or to taste

I tablespoon soy sauce

20 lumpia wrapper triangles
(see recipe page 108)

Directions continued on page 110.

Using 2 tablespoons of the oil, stir-fry the meat, fish, or chicken for 3 to 4 minutes, or until browned in a large skillet or wok. If using pork, be sure to cook thoroughly. Set aside. To the drippings, add the onions and 2 or 3 vegetables of your choice. Sauté for 5 to 6 minutes, or until the onions are translucent and the vegetables are tender-crisp. If necessary, add another tablespoon of the oil. Fold the meat, fish, chicken, or tofu into the vegetables, adding the salt, pepper, and soy sauce. Stir over medium heat for 1 to 2 minutes, or until heated through. Remove from the heat, drain, and allow to cool.

One at a time, lay each wrapper flat. Place 1 tablespoon filling in the center of the wrapper. Fold in the corners to create a pouch. Seal the edges with a dab of water. Repeat until all 20 wrappers are folded. Fry the lumpia in the remaining oil for 3 to 4 minutes, or until golden brown. Be careful not to overcook. Serve with Simply Sauce (see recipe page 125).

BEEF LUMPIA

Beef and Potato Egg Roll

YIELDS 10

These Filipino egg rolls may be served fresh or fried. Purchase ready-made Chinese egg-roll or wonton wrappers in Asian supermarkets or make your own Round Wrappers (see recipe page 108).

To a large skillet, add the beef, 3 cloves garlic, onion, red pepper, carrot, and vegetable oil. Sauté for 4 to 5 minutes, or until the beef is browned, and the vegetables are crisp-tender. Stirring constantly, fold in the potatoes and cook over medium heat for 3 to 4 minutes, or until the potatoes are heated through.

One at a time, lay each round wrapper flat. Place 2 tablespoons filling in the center of wrapper. Roll up, seal the edges with a dab of water, and place edges down. Serve warm with mounds of the remaining minced garlic and Lumpia Dipping Sauce (see recipe page 126).

1 pound ground beef

18 cloves garlic, minced

1 medium onion, minced

1 red pepper, diced

1 carrot, peeled and shredded

1 tablespoon vegetable oil

2 medium potatoes, parboiled and finely diced

10 (5-inch) round lumpia wrappers

Tip: Handle lumpia wrappers gently and work quickly because they dry out and tear easily. Cover the wrappers with a moist paper towel while working.

Minced Beef and Raisin Egg Rolls

YIELDS 20

Premade lumpia wrappers are available in Asian supermarkets.

Brown the beef and set aside. To the drippings, add the onions and sauté to a golden brown. If necessary, add a tablespoon of the oil. Fold the beef into the onions, adding the soy sauce, salt, and pepper. Stir in the raisins and allow to cook for 1 to 2 minutes, or until heated through. Remove from the heat, drain, and allow to cool.

One at a time, lay each wrapper triangle flat. Place 1 tablespoon filling in the center of the wrapper. Fold in the corners to create a pouch. Repeat until all 20 wrappers are folded. Fry the lumpia in ¼ inch oil for 3 to 4 minutes, or until golden brown. Be careful not to overcook.

1 pound chopped beef

4 small onions, diced

1 tablespoon soy sauce

½ teaspoon salt,
or to taste

⅛ teaspoon pepper,
or to taste

1 cup raisins

20 lumpia wrapper
triangles
(see recipe page 108)

½ cup vegetable oil

Green Peppers and Beef Egg Rolls

YIELDS 20

Pepper (paminta) *is a popular seasoning in the Philippines. The difference between white and black pepper is that the less pungent white pepper is ground from black peppercorns whose skins have been removed. Premade lumpia wrappers are available in Asian supermarkets.*

Using a wok or large skillet, stir-fry the beef and onion in the vegetable oil for 1 to 2 minutes, or until the beef is brown. Add the green pepper, salt, garlic powder, carrot, and pepper; stir-fry for 1 to 2 minutes, or until the vegetables are crisp-tender. Remove from the heat.

One at a time, lay each wrapper triangle flat. When cool enough to handle, place 1 tablespoon filling in the center of the wrapper. Fold in the corners to create a pouch. Repeat until all 20 wrappers are folded. Fry the lumpias in ¼ inch oil for 3 to 4 minutes, or until golden brown. Be careful not to overcook.

1 pound lean hamburger

½ cup minced onion

1 tablespoon vegetable oil

½ cup minced green pepper

¼ teaspoon salt,
or to taste

¼ teaspoon garlic powder

1 medium carrot, peeled
and grated

¼ teaspoon ground white
pepper

20 lumpia wrapper
triangles
(see recipe page 108)

½ cup vegetable oil

Surf and Turf Egg Rolls

YIELDS 20

Premade lumpia wrappers are available in Asian supermarkets.

Sauté the beef in 1 tablespoon vegetable oil in a large skillet or wok for 3 to 4 minutes, or until the pinkness is gone. Drain the excess grease. Add the shrimp, onion, water chestnuts, bamboo shoots, celery, garlic, and carrot. Stir-fry for 3 to 4 minutes, or until the carrot is tender-crisp. Add the bean sprouts, raisins, salt, and pepper. Stir-fry for 1 to 2 minutes, or just until the bean sprouts are limp. Spoon the mixture into a strainer and cool, allowing as much liquid as possible to drain before filling the wrappers.

One at a time, lay each wrapper triangle flat. When cool enough to handle, place 2 tablespoons filling in the center of the wrapper. Fold in the corners to create a pouch. Seal the edges with a drop of water. Repeat until all 20 wrappers are folded. Fry the lumpias in the remaining oil for 3 to 4 minutes, or until golden brown. Be careful not to scorch.

1 pound ground round beef

½ cup vegetable oil

½ pound raw shrimp, shelled and minced

1 medium onion, minced

1 (8-ounce) can water chestnuts, drained and minced

1 (4-ounce) can bamboo shoots, drained and minced

1 stalk celery, finely chopped

3 cloves garlic, minced

1 medium carrot; grated or finely chopped

1 pound fresh bean sprouts, chopped

½ cup raisins, chopped

½ teaspoon salt, or to taste

½ teaspoon pepper, or to taste

20 lumpia wrapper triangles
(see recipe page 108)

Vegetable Beef Egg Rolls

YIELDS 40

Premade lumpia wrappers are available in Asian supermarkets.

In a large skillet or wok, combine the ground meat, onion, and 2 tablespoons oil. Stir-fry over medium-high heat for 1 to 2 minutes, or until the meat is thoroughly done. Add the carrots first, stir-frying for 1 to 2 minutes. Add the cabbage, green beans, and bean sprouts, stir-frying for 3 to 4 minutes, or until the vegetables are crisp-tender. Add the cilantro, garlic powder, and soy sauce. Drain off any liquid that is not absorbed by the mixture. Remove from the heat, and set aside until cool enough to handle.

One at a time, lay each wrapper triangle flat. Place 1 tablespoon filling in the center of the wrapper. Fold in the corners to create a pouch. Repeat until all 20 wrappers are folded.

Heat the remaining oil to 375° F and deep-fry the lumpia, a few at a time, for 3 to 4 minutes, or until golden brown. Be careful not to overcook.

1 pound ground beef or pork

1 onion, thinly sliced

¾ cup vegetable oil

3 carrots, peeled and shredded

2 cups coarsely shredded cabbage

2 cups diagonally sliced green beans

2 cups bean sprouts

¼ cup chopped fresh cilantro

½ teaspoon garlic powder

¼ cup soy sauce

40 lumpia wrapper triangles
(see recipe page 108)

Beef Egg Rolls

YIELDS 40

Premade lumpia wrappers are available in Asian supermarkets.

In a large skillet or wok, combine the ground meat, onion, and 2 tablespoons oil. Stir-fry over medium-high heat for 1 to 2 minutes, or until the meat is thoroughly done. Add the salt, garlic, cabbage, flour, and pepper, stir-frying for 5 to 6 minutes, or until the cabbage is crisp-tender. Drain off any liquid that is not absorbed by the mixture. Remove from the heat, and set aside until cool enough to handle.

One at a time, lay each wrapper triangle flat. Place 1 tablespoon filling in the center of the wrapper. Fold in the corners to create a pouch. Repeat until all 40 wrappers are folded.

Heat the remaining oil to 375° F and deep-fry the lumpia, a few at a time, for 3 to 4 minutes, or until golden brown. Be careful not to overcook.

1 ½ pounds ground beef

1 green onion,
thinly sliced

¾ cup vegetable oil

¼ teaspoon salt,
or to taste

2 cloves garlic, minced

3 cups very finely chopped
cabbage or bok choy

2 tablespoons flour

⅛ teaspoon pepper,
or to taste

40 lumpia wrapper
triangles
(see recipe page 108)

Ground Round Triangles

YIELDS 40

Premade lumpia wrappers and patis *are available in Asian supermarkets.*

In a wok or saucepan, sauté the beef, garlic, and onion in 3 tablespoons oil for 6 to 7 minutes, or until the beef is brown and the onion is translucent. Add the water chestnuts, bean sprouts, mushrooms, salt, pepper, and *patis*; simmer for 2 to 3 minutes. Drain, reserving the juice, and cool thoroughly.

One at a time, lay each wrapper triangle flat. Place 1½ tablespoons filling in the center of the wrapper. Roll tightly, folding in wrapper ends to create a pouch. Moisten the edges lightly with water to seal. Repeat until all 40 wrappers are folded. Fry the lumpia in the remaining 5 tablespoons vegetable oil for 3 to 4 minutes, or until golden brown. Be careful not to scorch. Serve with Paalat Lumpia Sauce (see recipe page 126).

1 pound ground round

2 cloves garlic, minced

1 large onion, coarsely chopped (1½ cups)

½ cup vegetable oil

1 (8-ounce) can water chestnuts, coarsely chopped

2 pounds bean sprouts

1 cup sliced fresh shiitake mushrooms

1½ teaspoons salt, or to taste

¼ teaspoon ground black pepper, or to taste

1 tablespoon *patis* (fish sauce) or soy sauce

40 lumpia wrapper triangles (see recipe page 108)

PORK LUMPIA

Deep-Fried Pork and Shrimp Lumpia with Jicama

YIELDS 20

Filipinos often use ground pork instead of ground beef. It definitely adds a certain flavor, but it presents a challenge, too. Pork has to be cooked thoroughly, but pan-frying or deep-frying egg rolls do not always allow for even cooking on the inside and out.

How do you avoid burning the outside while thoroughly cooking the inside of the egg roll? Try this "old Filipino secret." If the wrapper is a deep golden brown, and yet the pork inside the lumpia is still pink, finish the cooking process in the microwave.

Combine the pork, shrimp, mushrooms, jicama, green onions, egg yolks, soy sauce, salt, and pepper in a mixing bowl.

One at a time, lay each wrapper triangle flat. Place 1½ tablespoons filling in the center of the wrapper. Roll tightly, folding in wrapper ends to create a pouch. Moisten the edges lightly with water to seal. Repeat until all 20 wrappers are folded. Fry the lumpias in ¼ inch oil for 3 to 4 minutes, or until golden brown. Be careful not to scorch. Serve with Sweet and Sour Sauce (see recipe page 128).

½ pound ground pork

½ pound raw shrimp, minced

½ cup minced fresh mushrooms

½ cup peeled and coarsely chopped jicama

2 green onions, finely sliced

3 egg yolks

2 tablespoons soy sauce

1 teaspoon salt, or to taste

¼ teaspoon ground black pepper, or to taste

20 lumpia wrapper triangles
(see recipe page 108)

½ cup vegetable oil

Pork and Bamboo Lumpia

YIELDS 20

Premade lumpia wrappers are available in Asian supermarkets.

Sauté the pork in 1 tablespoon vegetable oil in a large skillet or wok for 3 to 4 minutes, or until the pinkness is gone, and it is thoroughly cooked. Drain the excess grease. Add the shrimp, onion, water chestnuts, bamboo shoots, celery, garlic, and carrot. Stir-fry for 3 to 4 minutes, or until the carrot is tender-crisp. Add the bean sprouts, raisins, salt, and pepper. Stir-fry for 1 to 2 minutes, or just until the bean sprouts are limp. Spoon the mixture into a strainer and cool, allowing as much liquid as possible to drain before filling the wrappers.

One at a time, lay each wrapper triangle flat. When cool enough to handle, place 2 tablespoons filling in the center of the wrapper. Fold in the corners to create a pouch. Seal the edges with a drop of water. Repeat until all 20 wrappers are folded. Fry the lumpias in the remaining oil for 3 to 4 minutes, or until golden brown. Be careful not to scorch. Serve with Chili Pepper–Pineapple Sauce (see recipe page 127).

Variations:
Garlic Shrimp and Bamboo Lumpia: eliminate the pork and increase the shrimp to 1½ pounds.

1 pound chopped pork

½ cup vegetable oil

½ pound raw shrimp, shelled and minced

1 medium onion, minced

1 (8-ounce) can water chestnuts, drained and minced

1 (4-ounce) can bamboo shoots, drained and minced

1 stalk celery, finely chopped

3 cloves garlic, minced

1 medium carrot, grated or finely chopped

1 pound fresh bean sprouts, chopped

½ cup raisins, chopped

½ teaspoon salt, or to taste

½ teaspoon pepper, or to taste

20 lumpia wrapper triangles (see recipe page 108)

Deep-Fried Pork and Shrimp Lumpia with Lemongrass

YIELDS 40

Lemongrass (tanglad in Tagalog) is a wonderfully lemon-scented grass with a bulbous stem and long layered stalk. Only the lower 3 inches are used. Grown for its fragrance and flavor, lemongrass is peeled, chopped, and pounded to release its essence before adding to recipes. Lemongrass and lumpia wrappers are available in Asian supermarkets.

In a wok or saucepan, sauté the pork, shrimp, garlic, green onions, onion, and lemongrass in 3 tablespoons oil for 6 to 7 minutes, or until the pork is thoroughly cooked, and the onion is translucent. Add the water chestnuts, bean sprouts, egg, salt, pepper, and soy sauce; simmer for 2 to 3 minutes. Drain, if necessary, and cool thoroughly.

One at a time, lay each wrapper triangle flat. Place 1½ tablespoons filling in the center of the wrapper. Roll tightly, folding in wrapper ends to create a pouch. Moisten the edges lightly with water to seal. Repeat until all 40 wrappers are folded. Use the remaining vegetable oil to fry the lumpias in ¼ inch oil for 3 to 4 minutes, or until golden brown. Be careful not to scorch. Serve with Lumpia Sauce (see recipe page 125).

½ pound ground pork

½ pound raw shrimp, peeled and minced

2 cloves garlic, minced

2 green onions, finely sliced

1 small onion, minced

2 tablespoons finely chopped lemongrass

½ cup vegetable oil

1 (8-ounce) can water chestnuts, coarsely chopped

½ pound fresh bean sprouts, chopped

1 egg, slightly beaten

½ teaspoons salt, or to taste

¼ teaspoon ground black pepper, or to taste

1 tablespoon soy sauce

40 lumpia wrapper triangles (see recipe page 108)

Pork and Vegetable Lumpia

YIELDS 40

Premade lumpia wrappers and patis *are available in Asian supermarkets.*

In a wok or saucepan, sauté the pork, garlic, and onion in 3 tablespoons oil for 6 to 7 minutes, or until the pork is thoroughly cooked, and the onion is translucent. Add the water chestnuts, bean sprouts, salt, pepper, and *patis*; simmer for 2 to 3 minutes. Drain, if necessary, and cool thoroughly.

One at a time, lay each wrapper triangle flat. Place 1½ tablespoons filling in the center of the wrapper. Roll tightly, folding in wrapper ends to create a pouch. Moisten the edges lightly with water to seal. Repeat until all 40 wrappers are folded. Fry the lumpias in ¼ inch of the remaining vegetable oil for 3 to 4 minutes, or until golden brown. Be careful not to scorch. Serve with Lumpia Sauce (see recipe page 125).

- 1 pound chopped or ground pork
- 2 cloves garlic, minced
- 1 large onion, coarsely chopped
- ½ cup vegetable oil
- 1 (8-ounce) can water chestnuts, coarsely chopped
- 2 pounds bean sprouts
- 1½ teaspoons salt, or to taste
- ¼ teaspoon ground black pepper
- 1 tablespoon *patis* (fish sauce) or soy sauce
- 40 lumpia wrapper triangles (see recipe page 108)

SHRIMP LUMPIA

Shrimp and Vegetable Wraps

4 TO 6 SERVINGS

Enjoy this Filipino version of the spring roll. Lumpia wrappers and bamboo shoots are available in Asian supermarkets.

Warm the oil in a large skillet over medium heat. Sauté the onion and garlic for 2 or 3 minutes, or until tender. Add the shrimp and pork, and cook for 8 to 10 minutes, or until the shrimp is pink and the pork is thoroughly cooked.

Stir in the bamboo shoots, carrots, and green beans. Sauté for 3 to 4 minutes, or until the vegetables are tender-crisp. Season to taste with salt and pepper.

To assemble the lumpia, place a single wrapper flat on a clean surface. Place a lettuce leaf on the wrapper. Spoon about one-quarter cup of the filling onto the lettuce leaf. Fold the lower half of the wrapper over the filling, overlapping the sides to enclose the filling. Seal the wrap with a dab of water on the edges. Serve warm with Lumpia Sauce (see recipe page 125).

1 tablespoon vegetable oil

½ medium onion, diced

2 cloves garlic, minced

3 ounces raw shrimp, shelled and deveined

2 ounces boneless pork

½ cup drained and julienned bamboo shoots

¼ cup julienned carrots

¼ cup julienned green beans

½ teaspoon salt, or to taste

⅛ teaspoon freshly ground black pepper

4 to 6 round (pre-cooked) lumpia or spring-roll wrappers

4 to 6 lettuce leaves

Garlic Shrimp and Bamboo Egg Rolls

YIELDS 20

Premade lumpia wrappers are available in Asian supermarkets.

Sauté the pork in 1 tablespoon vegetable oil in a large skillet or wok for 1 to 2 minutes, or until opaque. Add the onion, water chestnuts, bamboo shoots, celery, garlic, and carrot. Stir-fry for 3 to 4 minutes, or until the carrot is tender-crisp. Add the bean sprouts, raisins, salt, and pepper. Stir-fry for 1 to 2 minutes, or just until the bean sprouts are limp. Spoon the mixture into a strainer and cool, allowing as much liquid as possible to drain before filling the wrappers.

One at a time, lay each wrapper triangle flat. When cool enough to handle, place 2 tablespoons filling in the center of the wrapper. Fold in the corners to create a pouch. Seal the edges with a drop of water. Repeat until all 20 wrappers are folded. Fry the lumpias in the remaining oil for 3 to 4 minutes, or until golden brown. Be careful not to scorch. Serve with Chili Pepper–Pineapple Sauce (see page 127).

1 ½ pounds raw shrimp, shelled and minced

½ cup vegetable oil

1 medium onion, minced

1 (8-ounce) can water chestnuts, drained and minced

1 (4-ounce) can bamboo shoots, drained and minced

1 stalk celery, finely chopped

3 cloves garlic, minced

1 medium carrot, grated or finely chopped

1 pound fresh bean sprouts, chopped

½ cup raisins, chopped

½ teaspoon salt, or to taste

½ teaspoon pepper, or to taste

20 lumpia wrapper triangles (available in Asian supermarkets or see Wrapper Triangles recipe page 108)

Chicken Lumpia with Water Chestnuts

YIELDS 40

Lumpia and patis *are available in Asian supermarkets.*

In a wok or saucepan, sauté the chicken, garlic, and onion in 3 tablespoons oil for 6 to 7 minutes, or until the chicken is brown and the onion is translucent. Add the water chestnuts, bean sprouts, salt, pepper, and *patis*; simmer for 2 to 3 minutes. Drain, if necessary, and cool thoroughly.

One at a time, lay each wrapper triangle flat. Place 1½ tablespoons filling in the center of the wrapper. Roll tightly, folding in wrapper ends to create a pouch. Moisten the edges lightly with water to seal. Repeat until all 40 wrappers are folded. Fry the lumpias in ¼ inch of the remaining vegetable oil for 3 to 4 minutes, or until golden brown. Be careful not to scorch. Serve with Lumpia Sauce (see recipe page 125).

I pound chopped or ground chicken

2 cloves garlic, minced

I large onion, coarsely chopped (1½ cups)

½ cup vegetable oil

I (8-ounce) can water chestnuts, coarsely chopped

2 pounds bean sprouts

1½ teaspoons salt, or to taste

¼ teaspoon ground black pepper

I tablespoon *patis* or soy sauce

40 lumpia wrapper triangles (see recipe page 108)

Lumpia Sauce

I CUP

Blend the cornstarch and brown sugar together in a small saucepan. Stir in 3 tablespoons water, the pineapple juice, soy sauce, and vinegar.

Bring the mixture to a boil over moderate heat, stirring frequently. Boil for 2 minutes to thicken.

Meanwhile, sauté the garlic in the oil for 2 or 3 minutes, or until golden brown. Add the garlic to the sauce and serve with the lumpia.

I tablespoon cornstarch

$\frac{1}{4}$ cup firmly packed brown sugar

$\frac{1}{4}$ cup pineapple juice

I tablespoon soy sauce

I tablespoons vinegar

2 cloves garlic, minced

I tablespoon vegetable oil

Simply Sauce

I CUP

Whip together 3 ingredients, and you have a quick, zesty sauce for dipping.

Combine the three ingredients. Allow to stand at room temperature for an hour. Use as a dipping sauce for lumpia.

$\frac{1}{2}$ cup soy sauce

$\frac{1}{2}$ cup white vinegar

2 cloves garlic, minced

Lumpia Dipping Sauce

2 CUPS

In a saucepan, combine the cornstarch, sugar, and soy sauce with 1½ cups water. Stirring constantly, cook over medium heat for 4 to 5 minutes, or until thickened. Serve hot.

¼ **cup cornstarch**

¼ **cup firmly packed raw or brown sugar**

¼ **cup soy sauce**

Paalat Lumpia Sauce

2 CUPS

Blend the sugar, soy sauce, broth, and salt in a saucepan over medium heat. Bring to a boil, then lower the heat to a simmer. Combine the cornstarch with 2 tablespoons cold water. Add 2 tablespoons hot broth to the cornstarch mixture, and then briskly stir the cornstarch mixture into the broth. Simmer for 2 to 3 minutes, stirring constantly, or until the sauce thickens. Sprinkle with the minced garlic and serve as a dipping sauce.

½ **cup firmly packed raw or brown sugar**

1 tablespoon soy sauce

2 cups beef broth or reserved juice from the Ground Round Triangles (see recipe page 117)

1 teaspoon salt, or to taste

2 tablespoons cornstarch

6 cloves garlic, minced

Chili Pepper-Pineapple Sauce

1 1/2 CUPS

Combine all but 1 tablespoon of the pineapple juice with the tomato paste, vinegar, sugar, chili pepper, ginger, and salt in a nonaluminum saucepan. Stir over medium heat for 3 to 4 minutes, or just until the mixture begins to boil. Reduce the heat.

Meanwhile, mix the cornstarch with the reserved pineapple juice to form a smooth paste. Add a tablespoon of the hot mixture to the paste. Then spoon the cornstarch into the hot mixture, stirring constantly to avoid lumps, and simmer over low heat for 3 to 4 minutes, or until the sauce has thickened.

1 cup pineapple juice

1/4 cup tomato paste

1/2 tablespoon apple cider vinegar

1 tablespoon raw or brown sugar

1 red chili pepper, minced

1/2 tablespoon minced ginger

1/4 teaspoon salt, or to taste

1 tablespoon cornstarch

Sweet and Sour Sauce

1 1/2 CUPS

Sweet and sour flavors originate from any number of food combinations. The sweet can come from sugar (palm, white, raw, or brown) or fruit juice (orange, pineapple, sweet mango, papaya, or rambutan, a close cousin of the lychee). The sour is produced from vinegar, unripe tamarind, or kamias *(a sour native fruit), lime or lemon juice, or sour fruit (green mango or guava). Try mix-matching various sweet and sour flavors to come up with your own unique sauce.*

Combine the vinegar, soy sauce, sugar, pineapple juice, ginger, and garlic in a nonaluminum saucepan. Bring to a boil, then lower the heat. Make a paste of the cornstarch and 2 tablespoons cold water. Vigorously stir the cornstarch paste into the sauce, and simmer for 5 to 6 minutes, or until thickened. Add salt to taste and serve warm as a dipping sauce.

1/4 cup apple cider vinegar

1 tablespoon soy sauce

1/2 cup firmly packed raw or brown sugar

1 cup pineapple juice

1/2 teaspoon minced ginger

1 clove garlic, minced

2 tablespoons cornstarch

1/2 teaspoon salt, or to taste

BARBECUE

As the story goes, American soldiers first brought barbecues to the Philippines in the 1940s. These delectable dinners did not take long to become a national obsession. Pork barbecue is the most popular, hacked into thick chunks and hoisted on wooden brochettes. The meat is usually brushed with a sweet and sour sauce that blends well with the faint smoky taste and pleasantly charred pork. Boneless chicken pieces are almost as popular, while steaks and pork chops are flame-grilled to provide the tastiest of meals.

Pineapple Teriyaki Barbecue Sauce

3 CUPS

This easy-to-make sauce is versatile enough to be used for any kind of meat or chicken. The unexpected surprise is that pineapple juice is a natural tenderizer.

Combine the ingredients. Use immediately, or refrigerate in a covered container for up to 1 week. Use it for barbecuing or broiling.

2 cups pineapple juice

¼ cup soy sauce

¼ cup palm or white vinegar

¼ cup firmly packed raw or brown sugar

¼ cup teriyaki sauce

1 tablespoon garlic powder

½ tablespoon cracked black pepper, or to taste

Pineapple Barbecued Chicken

8 SERVINGS

Pierce the chicken pieces with a fork for them to better absorb the sauce. Combine the chicken and sauce in a 9 by 13-inch container, stirring to evenly coat, and refrigerate. Marinate for at least 2 hours or overnight.

3 pounds chicken breast pieces

3 cups Pineapple Teriyaki Barbecue Sauce (see recipe page 130)

Barbecue the chicken for 12 to 15 minutes, or until the chicken is tender. Brush additional sauce on the chicken while grilling, if desired. Test for doneness by piercing with a fork. If the chicken or juices are still pink, grill for another 1 to 2 minutes. Repeat the test. To serve the remaining sauce for dipping, microwave on high for 2 to 3 minutes, covered, and serve piping hot.

Variations:
Pineapple Barbecued Flank Steak: substitute 2 pounds flank steak for the chicken.

PORK

With the exception of Islamic western Mindanao and its religious edicts against eating pork, the people throughout the rest of the Philippines relish this succulent meat. Because of pork's popularity and versatility, recipes abound, from to hams to pork rind to pigs' feet. Nothing is wasted. The ultimate porcine experience is *Lechón* (roasted suckling pig), but barbecued pork is another local favorite. What is its Filipino twist? A dipping sauce made of vinegar and minced garlic.

The cooking methods, indigenous fruit, and, most of all, the mix of cultures that has influenced Filipino cuisine make for adventurous dining. On that note, experiment with some of the following recipes for preparing pork.

Pork Pot Roast in Lechón Sauce

Pork shoulder or pork butt are the cuts of choice in Paksiw na Lechón, *but any cut of pork may be used. The rich flavor of the* Lechón Sauce *comes from the unique combination of chicken liver, apple cider vinegar, and brown sugar.*

Combine all the ingredients in a 3-quart stainless steel, iron, or enamelware pot. (Vinegar reacts with aluminum.) Bring to a boil, cover, and lower the heat. Simmer for 2 hours, or until the pork is tender and thoroughly cooked. If necessary, add ½ cup water to prevent scorching. Remove the bay leaves and serve in a preheated tureen.

2 pounds roast pork shoulder,
cut into 1-inch cubes

¼ pound chicken liver, coarsely chopped

1 cup apple cider vinegar

½ cup dry bread crumbs

1 medium onion, minced

9 cloves garlic, minced

1 teaspoon fresh thyme

1 stick cinnamon

3 bay leaves

½ cup soy sauce

1 tablespoon coarsely ground black peppercorns

½ teaspoon salt, or to taste

¾ cup firmly packed brown sugar

Whole Suckling Pig

LECHÓN   **25 TO 30 SERVINGS**

Roast pork is a popular food in the Philippines, in fact so popular that the town of Balayan holds an annual parade in its honor. The Parada ng mga Lechón, *the biggest celebration in Balayan, coincides with celebration of the feast of St. John the Baptist each June 24. This parade presents elaborately prepared roasted pigs in keeping with the fiesta's annual theme. Each year,* lechóns *(roasted pigs) are contributed and "dressed" by the local townspeople. During the parade, residents and guests douse each other with water, adding to the festive atmosphere.*

Prepare the barbecue pit by digging a hole 2 to 3 feet deep by 2 feet wide. Line with stones. Use one 15-pound bag charcoal. Put two thirds of the charcoal in the bottom of the pit.

Have the butcher clean and trim the pig, being sure to remove the feet. Thoroughly rinse the pig. Place it in a soup pot or large crock and marinate with the vinegar for 1 hour, turning every 15 minutes.

Drain the pig, reserving 1 cup vinegar. Combine the salt, pepper, and granulated garlic. Rub the pig thoroughly inside and out with the mixture. Make tiny knife-slits in the surface of the skin and insert fresh garlic slivers.

1 whole (10-pound) suckling pig

1 quart white vinegar

2 cups salt, or to taste

2 tablespoons pepper, or to taste

4 tablespoons granulated garlic

12 cloves garlic, peeled and sliced

½ cup vegetable oil

Parsley sprigs

Wrap the pig in three layers of heavy-duty aluminum foil that are about 8 inches longer than the pig on both ends. Lightly grease the inside of the foil with oil. Fold the foil around the pig to make a package, rolling up the layers of foil at the seams to form a very tight seal all around. When the package is completely wrapped, enclose it again in another tight layer of foil.

Continued on page 136.

Start the charcoal in the bottom of the pit. When it begins to ash, cover it with a thin layer of medium-sized stones. Place the foil-wrapped pig on top. Surround it with the rest of the charcoal, and light the charcoal. When the second layer of charcoal becomes ashes, turn the pig, and fill in the hole with dirt. Allow the suckling pig to cook in the pit for 5 to 6 hours or longer for pigs that are larger than 10 pounds.

Dig up the pig; remove it to a platter with two tongs, and partially unwrap it. Test the pig to see if it is done. Cut into the thigh next to the bone; it should be very well done, white, with no pink showing, and it should pull off the bone easily. Check the rib cavity also to make sure that the meat is uniformly white, not pinkish, and shreds easily. The meat is done when the skin shows deep splits and it shows internal temperatures of 160 to 170° F. If it is underdone, rewrap the pig, and place it in a hot oven (400° F) for 1 hour, or until thoroughly cooked.

Place the pig on a preheated platter and surround with parsley sprigs. Carve and serve.

Chinese Ham

Place ham and 3 cups pineapple juice in a stockpot. Bring to a boil, cover, and lower the heat. Simmer for 1 hour and 15 minutes, or about 25 minutes per pound. Remove from the juice. When cool enough to handle, trim the excess fat.

Preheat the oven to 350° F. Combine the remaining 1 cup pineapple juice with the brown sugar. Place the ham in a roasting pan, and glaze it with the brown-sugar mixture. Bake for 30 to 40 minutes, or until the glazed ham is golden-brown. Garnish with pineapple rings. (Leftovers freeze well.)

1 (3-pound) leg cured Chinese ham

4 cups pineapple juice

2 cups firmly packed brown sugar

1 (6-ounce) can pineapple rings

Fiesta Ham with Rambutan-Lychee Glaze

24 SERVINGS

For a tasty treat from the islands, make this exotic but easy ham and fruit glaze for your next Sunday dinner. Serve with yams, fluffy rice, and yard-long beans for a Filipino feast. Rambutan and lychees are available in Asian supermarkets.

Preheat the oven to 325° F. Combine the wine and reserved pineapple syrup with ½ cup water. Bring to a boil. Add the salt, rambutan, lychees, drained pineapple, and mango-pineapple preserves. Gradually stir in 1 cup sugar. Simmer for 8 to 10 minutes, or until the rambutan and lychee are tender, and the mixture has a very thick consistency. Drain the syrup from the fruit mixture into a serving bowl and set aside.

Using a sharp knife, score the fat of the ham into a diamond pattern. Brush generously with ⅔ of the fruit glaze. Press a whole clove into the center of each diamond.

Place the ham in a roasting pan and bake for 1 hour, basting often with the pan juices.

After 1 hour, raise the oven temperature to 450° F. Bake, basting often, for 18 to 20 minutes. Brush the ham with the remaining fruit glaze. Sprinkle the remaining ¼ cup sugar on top of the ham, and bake until the surface is crisp and golden brown. Transfer to a prewarmed serving platter and serve.

½ cup chardonnay
or other white wine

1 (10-ounce) can
pineapple (reserve syrup)

½ teaspoon salt,
or to taste

½ cup fresh or canned
rambutan, meat only,
finely chopped

½ cup fresh or canned
lychees, finely chopped

3 tablespoons
mango-pineapple preserves

1¼ cups firmly packed
raw or brown sugar

1 (6- to 7-pound) ham,
cooked

¼ cup whole cloves

Pork Guisantes and Peas

6 SERVINGS

Patis *is available in Asian supermarkets.*

Heat the oil in large skillet. Sauté the onion, garlic, and pork for 7 to 8 minutes, or until the pork has browned. Add the soy sauce, *patis*, bay leaf, and ½ cup water. Bring to a boil, reduce the heat, cover, and simmer for 8 to 10 minutes, or until the pork is tender and thoroughly cooked. Add the tomato paste, peas, pimientos, and salt. Stirring occasionally, simmer for 5 to 8 more minutes, or until the tomato paste and juice has formed a smooth sauce.

2 tablespoons vegetable oil

1 medium onion, sliced

2 cloves garlic, minced

1½ pounds lean pork, sliced in 1-inch pieces

1 tablespoon soy sauce

2 tablespoons *patis*, or soy sauce

1 bay leaf

3 ounces tomato paste

1 (6-ounce) package frozen peas

1 (3-ounce) can pimientos, julienned

½ teaspoon salt, or to taste

Homemade Philippine Sausage

8 SERVINGS

This recipe for delectable cocktail or party sausages is not as hard to make as you might think. It requires only six ingredients. Purchase the sausage casings in any Asian or Filipino supermarket.

Combine the pork, vinegar, garlic, salt, and peppers. Mix well and stuff into the sausage casings. Twist every 1 to 2 inches to make links.

Prick the skin of each link with a fork. Add the sausages and 1 quart water to a 2-quart nonaluminum pan. Boil for 15 to 16 minutes, or until the pork is thoroughly cooked. Drain the water. Using the same pot, pan-fry the sausages in their own fat for 2 to 3 minutes on each side, or until they are a golden brown.

2 pounds chopped or ground pork

½ cup palm or apple cider vinegar

4 cloves garlic, minced

1 teaspoon salt, or to taste

½ teaspoon ground black pepper, or to taste

¼ teaspoon cayenne pepper, optional

Sausage casings

Pork Crackling

An authentic, inexpensive pulutan *or snack, pork crackling is a crowd-pleaser at parties. Serve these pork rinds with plenty of Garlic Vinegar Dipping Sauce (see recipe page 165).*

Slice the pork rind into 1-inch squares. Boil the rind with salt in 1 quart water for 25 minutes.

Preheat the oven to 300° F. Remove the pork rind from the water with a slotted spoon, drain, and arrange on a baking sheet so no pieces are touching. Bake for 3 hours. Remove from oven and cool.

2 pounds pork rind

1 tablespoon salt, or to taste

2 cups vegetable oil

Heat the vegetable oil in a deep pot and deep-fry small batches of pork rind over high heat for 1 to 2 minutes, or until they puff up. Remove with a slotted spoon and drain on paper toweling. Continue until all the pork rind has been deep-fried.

Lechón de Jamon

40 SERVINGS

Annatto powder is used to impart a reddish color to food. If annatto powder (also called achuete *or* achiote) *is unavailable, substitute either* 1/8 *teaspoon red food coloring or 2 teaspoons paprika.*

Rinse the ham in cold water. Pat dry and rub with salt. Cover and refrigerate overnight. Remove the salt by thoroughly rinsing ham with cold water. Pat dry and rub with annatto powder. Air dry for 2 to 3 hours on a rack in a roasting pan.

Combine the minced garlic, peppercorns, lemon juice, rum, milk, and olive oil to use as a basting sauce.

Preheat the oven to 400° F. Roast the ham for 3½ to 4 hours, or until the pork is thoroughly cooked (160 to 170° F). Baste every 30 minutes with the sauce. Rotate the pan for even browning. Reduce the temperature to 325° F after the first hour. Arrange heads of garlic around the ham during the last hour of roasting. Reserve the roasted garlic heads for the sauce. Serve hot with the Chicken Liver and Roasted Garlic Sauce (see recipe on page 143). If a spicier condiment is desired, serve with Habañera Sauce (see recipe on page 144).

1 (20-pound) fresh ham, not cured, not smoked

3 cups kosher salt

3 tablespoons annatto powder

5 cloves garlic, minced

1 tablespoon cracked black peppercorns

½ cup lemon juice

2 cups dark rum

2 cups milk

1 cup olive oil

9 heads fresh garlic

Chicken Liver and Roasted Garlic Sauce

3 CUPS

Extract the cooked cloves from the roasted garlic heads. Using a nonaluminum skillet, sauté the chicken liver and shallots in the olive oil for 3 to 4 minutes. Pour in the wine vinegar and mirin; simmer for 3 to 4 minutes. Mix in the roast garlic cloves and lechón drippings. Pureé in a blender or food processor. Serve hot, poured over the *Lechón de Jamon*.

9 heads fresh garlic, oven-roasted (see recipe on page 142)

2 pounds chicken liver, chopped

4 shallots, chopped

¼ cup olive oil

¼ cup wine vinegar

¼ cup *mirin* (Japanese sweet rice wine)

⅓ cup *Lechón de Jamon* drippings (see recipe on page 142)

Habañera Sauce

2 CUPS

Wearing gloves, finely chop the habañera peppers. Using a nonaluminum skillet, sauté the peppers, shallots, garlic, ginger, and plum tomatoes in the olive oil for 6 to 7 minutes. Stir in the rice vinegar, salt, and pepper, and simmer for 5 to 6 minutes. Turn the mixture into in a blender or food processor and purée. Use as an accompaniment to the *Lechón de Jamon* (see recipe on page 142).

Note: Habañera peppers are the hottest peppers in the world. Wear gloves when chopping the peppers. Do not touch your eyes or delicate membranes before washing your hands. Jalapeño or milder peppers can be used as a substitute.

4 habañera peppers

4 shallots, coarsely chopped

4 cloves garlic, minced

2 tablespoons minced ginger

6 plum tomatoes, diced

3 tablespoons olive oil

¼ cup rice wine vinegar

½ teaspoon salt, or to taste

¼ teaspoon ground black pepper, or to taste

Pigs' Knuckles

Paksiw is a Filipino method of cooking meat or fish in vinegar, garlic, and hot peppers.

Boil the pigs' knuckles and salt in 2 quarts water for 3 hours, or until tender. If using a pressure cooker, boil for 25 to 30 minutes. Remove and drain thoroughly.

Deep-fry the pigs' knuckles in 1 cup oil for 8 to 10 minutes, or until crisp and golden. Remove and drain. Using the remaining ¼ cup oil, sauté the garlic and tomatoes in a large, nonaluminum skillet. Add the pigs' knuckles, soy sauce, vinegar, black pepper, jalapeño pepper, and bay leaf. Cover and simmer for 20 to 25 minutes, or until the flavors have melded. Remove the bay leaf and serve steaming hot.

6 pigs' knuckles

1 tablespoon salt

1 ¼ cups vegetable oil

6 cloves garlic, minced

3 plum tomatoes, coarsely chopped

¼ cup soy sauce

¼ cup vinegar

1 teaspoon coarsely cracked black pepper, or to taste

1 jalapeño pepper

1 bay leaf

Grilled Pork

Inihaw is Tagalog for charcoal-grilled or broiled food. The following recipe may be broiled, but nothing brings out the flavor like charcoal grilling.

Combine all the ingredients in a nonaluminum container, stirring to coat all sides evenly. Cover and refrigerate overnight, turning once or twice to marinate equally.

If oven roasting, preheat oven to 450° F. Roast pork for 30 minutes, or until it is thoroughly done (170° to 185° F).

If char-broiling, grill pork for 15 minutes each side, or until it is thoroughly done (170° to 185° F).

8 (½-inch thick) pork chops or 16 pork spare ribs

1½ cups apple cider vinegar

6 cloves garlic, minced

⅔ cup packed brown sugar

1 tablespoon salt, or to taste

⅔ cup soy sauce

Halloween Blood Stew

DINUGUAN   4 SERVINGS

A nutritious and popular stew in the Philippines, this recipe might translate better to American tastes on October 31. Consider it for your next Halloween party. Patis *and pigs' blood are available in Asian supermarkets.*

Cover the pork with water and simmer for 30 minutes. Remove from broth; when cool enough to handle, dice the pork. Reserve 1½ cups of broth.

In a 2-quart nonaluminum saucepan, heat the oil and sauté the garlic and onion for 2 to 3 minutes, or until the onion is opaque. Add the diced pork, liver, patis, and salt. Sauté for 5 to 6 minutes.

Add the vinegar and bring to a boil without stirring. Lower heat and simmer, uncovered, until the liquid is reduced by half. Add the broth. Simmer for 9 to 10 minutes. Stir in the blood and sugar; simmer until the stew thickens, stirring occasionally to avoid curdling.

Add the hot banana peppers and oregano. Simmer for 5 minutes, and serve steaming hot.

1 pound pork

2 tablespoons vegetable oil

3 cloves garlic, minced (to keep away vampires?)

1 medium onion, diced

¼ pound pork liver, diced

2 tablespoons *patis* (fish sauce), or soy sauce

1 teaspoon salt, or to taste

½ cup red wine vinegar

1½ cups beef broth

1 cup frozen pigs' blood

2 teaspoons raw or brown sugar

3 hot banana peppers

¼ teaspoon fresh oregano (optional)

BEEF

Until the sixteenth century, when the Spanish arrived in the Philippines with domestic cattle, beef was virtually unknown. Small herds were maintained through the centuries, but it wasn't until the 1940s, when Americans brought their love of barbecues and steaks, that beef dishes began to catch on.

Although beef is growing in popularity, it not as popular as pork, except in southern Mindanao, where the Islamic influence prohibits pork. For the majority of Filipinos, pork, chicken, fish, and shellfish provide the basis for meals.

However, beef dishes with a Filipino twist such as *bistek* (pan-fried steak), oxtail stew, and *sinigang* offer delectable dining. Try beef the Filipino way!

Hearty Beef Stew

4 SERVINGS

Originally caldereta *was prepared with goat meat. Today beef, lamb, pork, or* chicken may be substituted. Siling labuyo *is available in Asian supermarkets*

Place the cubed meat in a bowl with the vinegar, salt, and pepper. Allow meat to marinate for 30 to 40 minutes. Reserving the liquid, drain the beef and pat dry.

Sauté the garlic, onion, tomatoes, green pepper, and 1 red pepper in the olive oil for 2 to 3 minutes. Add the drained beef cubes and liver cubes, and sauté for 3 to 4 minutes, or until the liver is done. Remove the liver with a slotted spoon, mash, and set aside.

Add the reserved vinegar mixture, beef bouillon, and tomato paste to the beef. Simmer over medium heat for 30 to 35 minutes, or until the meat is tender.

Fold in the pickles and olives. Wear gloves to coarsely chop the chilies and stir them into the mixture. Add the mashed liver, and simmer for 8 to 10 minutes, or until the sauce thickens. Stir in the light cream and grated cheese. Heat thoroughly and transfer to a pre-warmed platter. Garnish with the remaining julienned red pepper.

2 pounds beef sirloin, cut into 1-inch cubes

3 tablespoons distilled white vinegar

1 teaspoon salt

¼ teaspoon ground black pepper

2 tablespoons minced garlic

2 cups chopped onion

1½ cups chopped tomatoes

1 large green bell pepper, seeded and julienned

2 large red bell peppers, seeded and julienned

¼ cup olive oil

½ pound beef liver, cut into 1-inch cubes

3 cups beef bouillon

1 tablespoon tomato paste

½ cup coarsely chopped dill pickles

½ cup coarsely chopped green olives

3 *siling labuyo* (finger chilies), or habañeras peppers

½ cup light cream

½ cup grated Parmesan cheese

Pan-Fried Beef Steak

Marinate the steaks in the salt, pepper, lemon juice, and soy sauce for 4 to 8 hours, turning once or twice. Using a large skillet, pan-fry the steaks, 2 at a time, in 2 tablespoons of oil for 2 to 3 minutes on each side. Transfer the steaks to a heated platter.

Add the remaining 2 tablespoons vegetable oil to the skillet and pan-fry the onions for 2 to 3 minutes, or until tender-crisp. Pile the onions high atop the steaks and serve piping hot.

4 (½-inch-thick) top round steaks

½ teaspoon salt, or to taste

½ teaspoon pepper, or to taste

2 tablespoons lemon juice

1 tablespoon soy sauce, or to taste

4 tablespoons vegetable oil

2 cups thinly sliced onions

Oxtail Stew in Peanut Sauce

KARI-KARE   6 SERVINGS

Place the oxtail pieces and stewing beef in a 4-quart pot. Add 1 cup water, or enough to cover the meat. Bring to a boil, lower the heat, cover, and simmer for 1½ hours, or until the meat is tender. Remove the meat from the pot, and reserve 2 cups broth.

Heat the oil in a skillet and sauté the garlic and onion. Add the cooked meat, the reserved broth, and salt. Simmer for 13 to 15 minutes.

Stir in the peanut butter, and simmer, stirring often, for 5 to 6 minutes, or until the peanut butter has blended into the broth. Add the green beans and eggplant. Simmer for 8 to 10 minutes, stirring occasionally, or until the vegetables are tender-crisp. Serve in preheated bowls.

2½ pounds oxtails, cut into 2-inch lengths

½ pound stewing beef, cooked and cut into 2-inch lengths

2 tablespoons vegetable oil

2 cloves garlic, minced

1 medium onion, sliced

1½ teaspoons salt

3 tablespoons peanut butter

½ pound green beans, trimmed and cut diagonally

1 medium eggplant, cut into 8 pieces

Beef Steak for Two

Calamansi *is a Filipino variety of lime. The size of a pearl onion, it has a dark green skin with pale green flesh, and an aromatic, tart citrus flavor.*

Marinate the beef slices in the *calamansi* or lime juice, white pepper, and soy sauce for 4 to 8 hours, turning once or twice. Using a large skillet, pan-fry the beef slices in 2 tablespoons of oil for 1 to 2 minutes on each side. Transfer the beef to a heated platter.

Add the remaining 1 tablespoon vegetable oil to the skillet and pan-fry the onion rings for 2 to 3 minutes, or until tender-crisp. Pile the onions high atop the beef slices and serve piping hot.

½ pound boneless beef sirloin, thinly sliced

1 tablespoon *calamansi* or lime juice

1 teaspoon ground white pepper, or to taste

1 tablespoon light soy sauce

3 tablespoons vegetable oil

1 onion, thinly sliced into rings

Garlic-Rubbed Sirloin Steak

4 SERVINGS

Serve for brunch with Filipino Salsa (see recipe page 202), fried eggs, and mounds of Filipino Fried Rice (see recipe page 90).

Trim the steaks. Combine the salt, sugar, garlic, and black pepper. Rub evenly on both sides of the steaks and store covered (or in a plastic bag) overnight in the refrigerator. Broil for 2 to 3 minutes on each side, or until done to desired degree.

4 (about 1 pound total) sirloin steaks, sliced ⅛ inch thick

½ tablespoon salt, or to taste

¼ cup firmly packed raw or brown sugar

4 cloves garlic, minced

1 teaspoon cracked black pepper, or to taste

Curried Beef, Filipino-Style

6 SERVINGS

Using a 2-quart pot, sauté the onions, garlic, ginger, celery, and tomatoes in the oil until lightly brown. Add the beef, stir-frying constantly until coated for 10 minutes. Add beef broth. Bring to boil, and then simmer for 1½ hours, or until the meat is tender.

Combine the coconut milk with the flour and curry powder. Gradually stir into the beef mixture. Add the vinegar, sugar, salt, pepper, and peanut butter, stirring constantly until thickened. Fold in the red and green peppers and pineapple. Turn off the heat, cover, and allow the flavors to marry for 10 minutes. Serve hot with condiment bowls of chopped eggs, diced cucumbers, and mango and papaya slices.

2 medium onions, chopped

2 cloves garlic, minced

1 (1-inch) cube ginger

2 stalks celery,
coarsely chopped

2 large tomatoes,
finely chopped

2 tablespoons vegetable oil

1½ pounds beef, cubed

3 cups beef broth

2 cups coconut milk

1 tablespoon flour

2 tablespoons curry powder

1 tablespoon palm or
apple cider vinegar

1 tablespoon raw or
brown sugar

1 teaspoon salt,
or to taste

½ teaspoon pepper,
or to taste

1 tablespoon peanut butter

2 medium green peppers,
coarsely chopped

2 medium red peppers,
coarsely chopped

6 slices fresh pineapple,
quartered

6 hard-boiled eggs, minced

2 medium cucumbers,
diced

3 mangoes, sliced

1 medium papaya,
cut into ½-inch slices

Lemon-Pepper Marinated Sirloin

4 SERVINGS

Marinate the meat in the lemon juice, soy sauce, pepper, and salt for 3 hours, or overnight.

Sauté the onion rings in the oil until transparent. Transfer to a serving dish, leaving the oil in the skillet. Strain the meat, reserving the marinade. Add the meat to the skillet and stir-fry over high heat for 5 to 6 minutes, or until the steak is tender. Transfer the meat to a warmed serving platter. Add the marinade and ½ cup water to the skillet, bring to a boil, lower the heat, and simmer for 10 to 12 minutes. Spoon over the steak and onion rings.

2 pounds sirloin steak, cut into ¼-inch cubes

2 tablespoons lemon juice

3 tablespoons soy sauce

½ teaspoon ground black pepper

1 teaspoon salt, or to taste

2 medium onions, thinly sliced into rings

¼ cup vegetable oil

Beef Sinigang

Whether beef, fish, or shellfish is the basis for this stew, sinigang *is the classic dish of the Philippines. Sour fruit such as tamarind,* calamansi *(small Filipino lime) or* kamias *(sour fruit) lend a pleasingly tart flavor. Good substitutes for these souring agents are lime or lemon juice. Tamarind powder, star anise, and water spinach are available in Asian supermarkets.*

Add the beef ribs, tamarind powder, and star anise, if desired, to 1 quart boiling water in a large pot. Bring to a boil again, and simmer for 15 minutes. Add the tomatoes, onion, and taro. Lower the heat, and simmer for 15 to 20 minutes, or until the taro is tender. Add the water spinach, beans, soy sauce, and pepper. Cover and simmer for 2 to 3 minutes, or until the water spinach is wilted, and the beans are tender-crisp.

2 pounds beef ribs, cut into serving-size pieces

1 (1½-ounce) package tamarind powder or ½ cup lime or lemon juice

1 star anise, optional

6 plum tomatoes, coarsely chopped

1 large onion, minced

2 cups peeled and cubed taro

1 pound water spinach, cut into 2-inch segments

1 pound green or yard-long beans, cut into 2-inch segments

1 tablespoon soy sauce, or to taste

¼ teaspoon ground black pepper, or to taste

SEAFOOD

Because the Philippines is an archipelago composed of 7,100 islands, fish and crustaceans are the basis of many Filipino meals. Saltwater fish such as sardines, tuna, bonito, mackerel, *lapu-lapu* (grouper), *apahap* (snapper), and *banak* (mullet) abound in the surrounding seas. Freshwater fish are plentiful in the rivers, lakes, and streams. An advanced system of aquaculture provides a steady supply of *bangus* (milkfish), mudfish, catfish, carp, and tilapia, which are farmed in artificially created *palaisdaan* (fishponds) or flooded rice paddies.

Shellfish are also popular and plentiful. As many as eight species of spiny lobsters and sixteen species of crabs, jumbo rivers prawns, and shrimp of all sizes inhabit the waters.

Cooking methods for seafood include *kinilaw* or *kilawin*, in which the fish or seafood is marinated with palm vinegar and lime juice, flavored with onions, ginger, cilantro, and chili peppers, and served raw. *Inihaw* is the process of grilling over hot coals. *Sinigang* refers to stewing in bouillon with vegetables, and *paksiw* refers to cooking with vinegar. *Halabos* is a method of salting and steaming fish in its own juice.

Butterflied Shrimp
with Spinach and Walnuts

4 SERVINGS

Marinate the shrimp, 2 tablespoons sherry, and ginger in a covered bowl and refrigerate overnight, or for at least 1 hour. Mix the remaining 2 tablespoons sherry, chicken broth, soy sauce, tomato paste, cornstarch, vinegar, sugar, sesame oil, and cayenne pepper in small bowl.

Heat 2 tablespoons peanut oil in wok or large skillet over high heat. Add the walnuts and stir-fry for 1 to 2 minutes. Remove the walnuts, using a slotted spoon. Add the spinach to the wok and stir-fry for 1 to 2 minutes, or just until wilted. Divide the spinach among four warm plates. Add 2 tablespoons peanut oil, the bell peppers, and garlic to the wok and stir-fry for 2 to 3 minutes, or until the peppers are tender-crisp. Add the remaining 1 tablespoon peanut oil, shrimp mixture, and green onions. Stir-fry for 1 to 2 minutes, or until the shrimp are opaque. Divide the shrimp among the four plates of spinach. Pour the broth mixture into the wok, and simmer, stirring occasionally, for 2 to 3 minutes, or until the sauce is clear and thickened.

Drizzle the sauce over the shrimp. Sprinkle with the walnuts, and serve.

2 pounds large uncooked shrimp, shelled, deveined, and butterflied

¼ cup dry cooking sherry

2 tablespoons minced fresh ginger

½ cup chicken broth

2 tablespoons soy sauce

1 tablespoon tomato paste

1 tablespoon cornstarch

1 tablespoon rice vinegar or white wine vinegar

1 tablespoon raw or brown sugar

1 tablespoon sesame oil

¼ teaspoon cayenne pepper

⅓ cup peanut oil

2 tablespoons chopped walnuts

4 cups spinach, washed and trimmed

2 bell red peppers, cut into 1-inch squares

2 cloves garlic, minced

8 green onions, sliced diagonally into 1-inch pieces

Shrimp Sinigang

4 SERVINGS

Whether fish, shellfish, or beef is the basis for this stew, sinigang *is the classic dish of the Philippines. Sour fruit such as tamarind,* calamansi *(small Filipino lime) or* kamias *(sour fruit) stimulate the appetite. Substitute lime or lemon juice for these souring agents if they are unavailable. Tamarind powder and water spinach are available in Asian supermarkets.*

Combine the tamarind powder with 2 quarts water in a large pot. Heat over high heat until it comes to a boil.

Meanwhile, sauté the garlic, onion, and tomatoes in the oil for 3 to 4 minutes, or until the onion is translucent. Add to the tamarind water. Fold in the whole radishes and simmer for 3 minutes. Add the shrimp, serrano pepper, water spinach, soy sauce, and black pepper to the mixture. Simmer for 5 to 6 minutes, or until the shrimp are pink, and the spinach is tender-crisp. Ladle into prewarmed soup bowls and serve steaming hot.

Variation:
Grouper Sinigang: substitute grouper fillets for the shrimp.

1 (1½-ounce) package tamarind powder or ½ cup lime or lemon juice

3 cloves garlic, minced

1 large onion, minced

4 plum tomatoes, coarsely chopped

2 tablespoons vegetable oil

2 cups whole radishes, trimmed

2 pounds jumbo shrimp, shelled and cleaned

1 serrano pepper

2 pounds fresh water spinach or spinach

1 tablespoon soy sauce, or to taste

½ teaspoon ground black pepper, or to taste

Grilled Whitefish

With a sharp knife, cut along the back of the fish and remove the backbone. Rinse the fish. Then rub the fish inside and out with lemon slices, and sprinkle with the salt and pepper.

Combine the tomatoes, onions, and green onions. Stuff the fish with the mixture. Wrap in foil, and grill over live coals for 13 to 15 minutes on each side, or until the fish flakes easily with a fork. Serve with lemon wedges and parsley sprigs.

1 (2-pound) white fish, dressed

2 slices lemon

1 ½ teaspoons salt, or to taste

⅛ teaspoon pepper, or to taste

½ cup chopped tomatoes

¼ cup chopped onions

2 green onions, thinly sliced

1 lemon, sliced into 4 wedges

4 sprigs fresh parsley

Shrimp Fritters

4 SERVINGS

Annatto or achiote seeds are used in the Philippines to flavor food and imbue it with a reddish tint. Annatto powder or seeds may be purchased at any Asian or Hispanic food market. Use the powder or make your own annatto water or oil (recipes follow). Annatto powder and bagoong *are available in Asian supermarkets.*

Combine the eggs, cornstarch, baking powder, pepper, and either the annatto powder with 1 tablespoon water or the annatto water. Set aside.

Brown the pork in 1 tablespoon vegetable oil in a heavy skillet. Remove the pork to a large bowl and toss well with the bean sprouts, shrimp, and *bagoong*.

Using a tablespoon or two of oil at a time, heat it in the skillet over a medium heat. Heap 2 tablespoons of the shrimp mixture onto the skillet. Drizzle 2 tablespoons of the cornstarch batter over the mixture. Fry for 1 to 2 minutes, or until the fritter reaches a golden brown color. Flip over, and fry for 1 to 2 minutes on the reverse side. Remove fritter with a spatula, and drain on paper towels. Repeat until all the shrimp mixture and batter are used. Serve hot with Garlic Vinegar Dipping Sauce (see recipe page 165).

2 eggs, beaten

1 cup cornstarch

1 teaspoon fresh baking powder

½ teaspoon ground white pepper

1 teaspoon annatto powder or 1 tablespoon annatto water

½ pound ground pork

½ cup vegetable oil

1 cup bean sprouts, coarsely chopped

24 medium shrimp, shelled, deveined, and coarsely chopped

1 tablespoon *bagoong* (shrimp paste) or 1 tablespoon soy sauce

Annatto Water

4 TO 5 TEASPOONS

Combine the annatto seeds with the water. Crush the seeds with the back of a spoon to release the red color. Allow the annatto seeds' color to disperse for 30 minutes. Strain and discard the seeds.

1 teaspoon annatto or achiote seeds

4 teaspoons water

Annatto Oil

2 TO 3 TEASPOONS

Combine the annatto seeds with the oil. Crush the seeds with the back of a spoon to release the red color. Allow the annatto seeds' color to disperse for 15 to 30 minutes. Strain and discard the seeds.

1 teaspoon annatto or achiote seeds

2 teaspoons olive oil

Garlic Vinegar Dipping Sauce

Combine all the ingredients and mix thoroughly.

⅓ cup palm or
white vinegar

4 cloves garlic, minced

¼ cup soy sauce

½ teaspoon salt,
or to taste

¼ teaspoon ground black
pepper, or to taste

⅛ teaspoon cayenne
pepper, or to taste

Sweet and Sour Fish

LAPU-LAPU ESCABECHE   **6 TO 8 SERVINGS**

Sauté the lapu-lapu in 2 tablespoons oil for 4 to 5 minutes on each side, or until the fish is done and flakes easily with a fork. Set aside on a warm platter. Sauté the garlic, onion, and sweet peppers in the remaining 2 tablespoons oil for 5 to 6 minutes, or until the onions are opaque and the peppers are tender-crisp. Remove the vegetables and set aside.

Combine the soy sauce, vinegar, sugar, cornstarch, and black pepper with ⅓ cup water. Add to the saucepan and stir constantly over medium heat for 3 to 4 minutes, or until the mixture thickens into a gravy. Fold in the sweet pepper mixture and simmer for 2 to 3 minutes, or until the vegetables are heated through and evenly coated. Spoon the vegetables onto the platter, arranging them around the fish. Pour the gravy over all and garnish with lemon wedges and parsley sprigs. Serve hot.

1 large (2-pound) lapu-lapu, dressed

¼ cup vegetable oil

6 cloves garlic, minced

1 large onion, sliced

2 large sweet green peppers, julienned

2 large sweet red peppers, julienned

⅓ cup soy sauce

⅓ cup vinegar

⅓ cup firmly packed brown sugar

2 tablespoons cornstarch

¼ teaspoon ground black pepper, or to taste

2 lemons, cut into wedges

Parsley sprigs

Pickled Whitefish with Bitter Melon

4 SERVINGS

Bitter melon, or ampalaya *in Tagalog, looks like a pointed, neon-green cucumber with warty skin. Living up to its name, it is fairly bitter and is an acquired taste. However, some* herbolarios *purport it to be medicinal—even aphrodisiacal. According to Filipino folklore, the more bitter the vegetable, the more valuable it is medicinally. Bitter melon is available at Asian supermarkets.*

Cut the fish into 4 slices. Place the fish in a non-aluminum skillet. Add the vinegar, salt, ginger, peppers, and ¼ cup water. Cover and bring to a boil. Lower the heat, and simmer for 9 to 10 minutes, turning the fish once to cook evenly.

Using wide spatulas, carefully transfer the fish to a covered dish. Pour the broth over all, and refrigerate for 2 days to allow the flavors to marry.

Reheat the fish in a nonaluminum skillet over medium heat for 9 to 10 minutes, or until just heated though.

Discard the inner pith and red seeds of the bitter melon. Using only the green skin and outer membrane, coarsely chop the melon. Add ½ cup melon and the eggplant during the last 5 minutes of cooking, stirring occasionally. Divide the fish and vegetables among four pre-warmed plates, and serve hot.

1 (1½-pound) whitefish, dressed

½ cup palm or white vinegar

1½ teaspoons salt, or to taste

2 tablespoons minced ginger

2 tablespoons chopped hot banana peppers

1 small slice bitter melon

1 cup thinly sliced eggplant

Spicy Shrimp

Gambas *is a piquant and popular dish in Manila. Serve hot over rice and garnish with olives.* Calamansi *and* siling labuyo *are available at Asian supermarkets.*

Marinate the shrimp in the chili sauce, *calamansi*, salt, and pepper for 30 minutes.

Using a skillet, sauté the garlic in the oil for 1 to 2 minutes, or until golden brown. Remove the garlic with a slotted spoon. Add the marinated shrimp and stir-fry for 4 to 5 minutes, or until pink. Add the sliced *siling labuyo* and more chili sauce, if desired. Serve on a preheated platter. Garnish with the sautéed garlic.

Tip: Chili peppers (*sili*) are available in two varieties: the longer *siling mahaba* and the smaller *siling labuyo*. Rule of thumb: the redder the color, the hotter the flavor. To reduce the heat yet retain the flavor of the chilies, remove the seeds and membranes.

2 pounds jumbo shrimp, peeled and cleaned

¼ cup chili sauce, or to taste

1 tablespoon *calamansi* or lemon juice

½ teaspoon salt, or to taste

½ teaspoon ground black pepper, or to taste

½ cup minced garlic

½ cup olive oil

2 to 4 *siling labuyo* or jalapeño peppers, thinly sliced

Steamed Crab Stuffed with Fresh Coconut

6 SERVINGS

For variety, substitute a large Dungeness crab for the blue crabs and increase the cooking time to 12 to 15 minutes.

Using a steamer or stockpot, steam the crabs for 5 minutes. Carefully remove the crabs. Lift the top shells and set aside. Clean out the gills.

Sauté the shallots and garlic in the oil until lightly browned. Add the grated coconut, basil, jalapeño, and salt and sauté for 3 to 4 minutes over medium heat.

Stuff the crabs with the coconut mixture. Arrange the lime slices on top. Cover the crabs and coconut mixture with the crabs' top shells. Tie shut with string.

Steam the blue crabs for 7 to 10 minutes. Serve with garlic vinegar.

6 blue crabs

2 shallots, minced

2 cloves garlic, minced

1 tablespoon peanut oil

1 cup freshly grated coconut

1 tablespoon minced fresh basil

1 jalapeño pepper, sliced

½ teaspoon salt, or to taste

1 lime, sliced

½ cup Garlic Vinegar (recipe follows)

Garlic Vinegar

½ CUP

Combine the garlic and vinegar in a clean glass jar. Cover and refrigerate for 2 days. Strain the vinegar. Keeps up to 1 week.

2 cloves garlic, minced

½ cup white vinegar

Black Rice Paella

Black rice (pirurutong) is traditionally used in making Filipino desserts. However, the black rice, with its smoother texture and subtle flavor, makes a distinctive but delectable backdrop for the familiar seafood paella. If black rice is unavailable, substitute white rice. Patis *and coconut milk are available in Asian supermarkets.*

Bring 6 cups water to a boil. Add the clams and continue boiling for 5 to 6 minutes, or until the shells open. When cool enough to handle, discard the top shells, transfer the clams and lower shells to a bowl, and reserve 4 cups clam broth.

Rinse the black rice in cold water. Sauté the onion and carrot in 3 tablespoons olive oil in a 2-quart pot over medium heat. Stir in the rice and salt. Add the reserved clam broth and bring to a boil. Reduce the heat, cover, and simmer for 18 to 20 minutes, or until the water has been absorbed and the rice is nearly cooked.

24 littleneck or cherrystone clams

2 cups black rice (*pirurutong*)

1 small onion, diced

1 carrot, peeled and diced

6 tablespoons olive oil

1 teaspoon salt, or to taste

1 stalk (3 inches) fresh lemongrass, minced, or 1 tablespoon dried

3 cloves garlic, minced

3 shallots, minced

2 green chilies, chopped

2 tablespoons minced fresh ginger

2 leeks, sliced

½ pound fresh shiitake mushrooms, sliced

Sauté the lemongrass, garlic, shallots, chilies, ginger, leeks, mushrooms, tomatoes, eggplants, and long beans in 3 tablespoons olive oil in a wok or skillet. Add the shrimp, crabs, clams, scallops, and coconut milk and stir well. Season with *patis* and lemon juice.

Add the seafood to the rice, and simmer for 5 to 7 minutes, or until the flavors marry and the paella is heated through. Transfer to a large, preheated serving bowl.

2 plum tomatoes, diced

2 Chinese eggplants, cubed

5 long beans (*sitao*) or green beans, cut in 2-inch lengths

I pound large shrimp with heads

3 blue crabs, cleaned and cut in half

2 pounds sea scallops

I cup coconut milk

2 tablespoons *patis* (fish sauce), or soy sauce

3 tablespoons lemon juice

Seviche

6 TO 8 SERVINGS

Seviche is a popular dish in the Philippines, and for good reason. It is delicious and easy to fix. In fact, it requires no cooking at all! Vinegar and/or calamansi, *lemon, or lime juice "cook" the fish. Use any fresh shellfish, fish, or combination to create a different seviche recipe each time. Look for* calamansi *in Asian supermarkets.*

Use only the freshest shellfish or fish. Be sure to shell, clean, and devein shrimp or shellfish. Clean, skin, and bone the fish. Rinse thoroughly, pat dry, and coarsely chop the shellfish or fish.

If adding jalapeño peppers, keep in mind that the seeds and membranes contain the most heat. For a mild seviche, do not use jalapeño peppers. For a hot seviche, use only the green flesh. For a *caliente* seviche (very hot), include the seeds and minced membranes.

Combine all the ingredients. Mix well to equally distribute the vinegar and citrus juice, cover, and marinate in the refrigerator for 1 hour, stirring occasionally. Drain and serve in stemmed sherbet dishes or iced individual bowls.

2 pounds fish or shellfish (bluefish, sea bass, *tanguigue*, shrimp, lobster, conch)

1 to 2 jalapeño peppers, minced, optional

1 cup palm or white vinegar

6 tablespoons *calamansi*, lemon, or lime juice

5 cloves garlic, minced

¼ cup chopped fresh cilantro

1 cup minced onion

4 plum tomatoes, diced

2 tablespoons minced fresh ginger

4 green onions, thinly sliced

2 red bell peppers, cored, seeded and coarsely chopped

2 green bell peppers, cored, seeded and coarsely chopped

1 teaspoon salt, or to taste

½ teaspoon ground black pepper, or to taste

Clam Stew

4 SERVINGS

Look for water spinach in Asian supermarkets.

Using a 2-quart saucepan, add the ginger to 6 cups water and bring to a boil. Stir in the clam meat, papaya, salt, and pepper. Simmer for 8 to 10 minutes, or until the clams are tender. Add the water spinach and simmer for 1 to 2 minutes, or until it is wilted. Serve in preheated bowls.

Tip: Try winter melon in place of the green papaya for a sharper flavor. Experiment with watercress instead of the water spinach or spinach.

2 tablespoons grated fresh ginger

3 cups shelled clams

I cup cubed green papaya

I teaspoon salt, or to taste

½ teaspoon ground black pepper, or to taste

I pound water spinach or spinach, cut into I-inch lengths

Fried Oysters and Tomatoes

GUISADONG TALABA

4 SERVINGS

Using a large skillet, sauté the garlic and onion in the oil for 2 to 3 minutes, or until the onion is transparent. Stir in the tomatoes and simmer for 2 to 3 minutes. Add the oysters, cover, and, stirring occasionally, simmer for 10 to 12 minutes, or until the oysters are tender. Add the salt and pepper and serve at once.

3 cloves garlic, minced

I medium onion, chopped

2 tablespoons vegetable oil

3 small plum tomatoes, chopped

2 cups shelled oysters

I teaspoon salt, or to taste

½ teaspoon ground black pepper, or to taste

CHICKEN

With the exception of pork, chicken may be the first choice of Filipinos. In fact, chicken has been called the blank canvas of Philippine cuisine. Its own subtle taste readily absorbs the flavors of the seasonings or spices used in its preparation.

The Philippines' indigenous fruits and vegetables shape the underlying framework for its poultry recipes, but Spain's occupation introduced seasonings from the Iberian Peninsula. These include garlic, paprika, wine, and olive oil from Europe, as well as sweet and hot chili peppers, tomatoes, and corn from the Americas.

Because of the Philippines' location along the ancient spice route, many seasonings from the Spice Islands also made their way into Filipino poultry dishes: peppercorns, bay leaves, cinnamon, coriander, and curry mixtures.

China's influence on Filipino poultry recipes is found in star anise, ginger, and the ubiquitous soy sauce.

All combined, the vast array of seasonings and spices, in addition to the various culinary styles, make for an extraordinary selection of Filipino poultry recipes.

Roasted Pineapple Chicken Breasts

6 SERVINGS

Soy sauce, made from fermented soybeans, is used liberally in Filipino cooking. Light soy sauce is saltier and lighter in color. The black soy sauce (toyo) lends a heartier flavor and color to dishes.

Preheat the oven to 425° F. Place the chicken, skin side up, in a shallow roasting pan. Combine the pineapple juice, bay leaf, vinegar, and soy sauce, and pour over the chicken. Cover with aluminum foil and bake for 30 minutes. Uncover and bake 20 minutes more, basting frequently, or until nearly all the liquid has evaporated and the chicken is a rich, dark brown.

3 large chicken breasts, split

1 (6-ounce) can unsweetened pineapple juice

1 bay leaf

¼ cup palm or apple cider vinegar

¼ cup light soy sauce

Baked Sweet Sour Chicken, Philippine-Style

4 SERVINGS

Preheat the oven to 350° F. Place the chicken, skin side up, in a shallow roasting pan. Mix the garlic salt, salt, corn syrup, soy sauce, and vinegar. Pour it over the chicken, cover, and bake for 1 hour, or until the chicken is tender.

2 large chicken breasts, split

¼ teaspoon garlic salt, or to taste

¼ teaspoon salt, or to taste

2 tablespoons white corn syrup

¼ cup soy sauce

¼ cup palm or apple cider vinegar

Philippine Chicken Dinner for Two

2 SERVINGS

In the Philippines, vinegar (suka) comes in white, red, and black colors. It can be made from pineapple, nipa palm, kaong or sago palm, coconut, or sugar cane. If these are unavailable (check in Asian supermarkets), apple cider or white vinegar can be substituted.

Arrange the chicken in a large skillet. Combine the vinegar, soy sauce, garlic, and pepper; pour over the chicken. Cover tightly; simmer over low heat, turning the chicken several times, for 40 minutes, or until it is tender. Remove the chicken to a heated platter. Warm the bean sprouts in the sauce and serve over hot, fluffy rice.

1 boned chicken breast, split

3 tablespoons palm or apple cider vinegar

3 tablespoons light soy sauce

2 cloves garlic, minced

⅛ teaspoon pepper, or to taste

1 cup fresh mung bean sprouts

2 cups cooked rice

Fried Chicken, Philippine-Style

4 TO 6 SERVINGS

Using a 2-quart saucepan, simmer the chicken in the vinegar, garlic, salt, pepper, and 1 cup water for 20 to 22 minutes, or until almost done. Drain off all liquid and remove the chicken. Add the vegetable oil to the saucepan. Heat until smoking, add the chicken to the oil, and deep-fry the chicken for 5 to 6 minutes, or until golden brown. Drain the chicken thoroughly.

1 (3-pound) chicken, cut into serving-size pieces

¼ cup white vinegar

4 cloves garlic, crushed

½ teaspoon salt, or to taste

¼ teaspoon pepper, or to taste

1 cup vegetable oil

Six-Ingredient Filipino Chicken

4 TO 6 SERVINGS

Preparation time is 5 minutes!

Combine the soy sauce, vinegar, corn syrup, and garlic salt. Add the oil to a 2-quart pot, and arrange the chicken pieces on top. Spoon the soy sauce mixture over the chicken. Cover and simmer over low heat, turning the chicken several times, for 35 to 40 minutes, or until the chicken is tender. Add 1 to 2 tablespoons water, if necessary. Serve hot or chilled.

¼ cup soy sauce

¼ cup palm or apple cider vinegar

1 tablespoon light corn syrup

1 teaspoon garlic salt, or to taste

2 tablespoons vegetable oil

1 (2-pound) frying chicken, cut into 4 to 6 serving-size pieces

Chicken Fritada with Sweet Potatoes

8 SERVINGS

Here the flavors of chicken and pork are blended, but with a twist. It's the slivers of liver that lend the rich flavor to the fritada.

Sauté the garlic in oil until golden brown. Add the onions and tomatoes. Simmer over low heat for 3 to 4 minutes, gradually adding 2 cups of water or until a sauce is formed. Add the chicken, pork, salt, and pepper. Bring to a boil, then lower the heat, and simmer for 20 to 25 minutes.

Add the sweet potatoes, red pepper, and liver. Simmer for 25 to 30 minutes, or until the pork is thoroughly cooked, and the chicken and vegetables are tender. Add more water, if necessary. Serve hot over white rice.

6 cloves garlic, minced

2 tablespoons vegetable oil

2 medium onions, thinly sliced

2 medium tomatoes, thinly sliced, or ½ cup tomato sauce

1 (2-pound) spring chicken, cut into 4 to 6 serving-size pieces

½ pound lean pork, cut into 1-inch cubes

1 tablespoon salt, or to taste

½ teaspoon ground white pepper, or to taste

2 medium sweet potatoes

1 sweet red pepper, quartered

2 ounces pork liver, julienned

8 cups cooked white rice

Roasted Chicken with Star Fruit and Hot Peppers

4 TO 6 SERVINGS

When purchasing star fruit, also called carambola, choose fruit that is uniformly yellow to orange and has a subtle aroma. If green, it is unripe and will lend very little flavor to the recipe, but when ripe, the flavor of star fruit bursts with a uniquely tropical blend of apple, banana, and lychee.

Rinse chicken well and pat dry.

In a 9 by 13-inch glass or ceramic baking pan, combine the olive oil, lime juice, zest, onions, honey, ginger, and pepper. Add three-fourths of the star fruit slices and the chicken, turning to coat evenly. Cover and refrigerate overnight, turning the chicken occasionally so it marinates uniformly.

Preheat the oven to 375° F. Season the chicken with salt. Sprinkle with almonds and bake for 35 to 40 minutes, basting frequently with pan juices and turning any chicken pieces that brown too quickly. Add the remaining star fruit slices, stir, and continue cooking for 15 to 20 minutes, or until the chicken is golden brown and a pierced thigh yields clear juices. Spoon sauce over the chicken, garnish with cilantro and serve hot from the oven.

*Tip: For a milder dish, discard the serrano or jalapeño seeds. For a spicier version, include the pepper seeds.

1 (3- to 3½-pound) chicken, cut into serving-size pieces

¼ cup olive oil

¼ cup freshly squeezed lime juice

½ cup minced lime zest

2 small onions, peeled and thinly sliced

¼ cup honey

1 tablespoon minced fresh ginger

1 serrano or jalapeño pepper, minced*

4 (4-ounce) star fruit, sliced crosswise

½ teaspoon salt, or to taste

½ cup chopped raw almonds

1 cup chopped fresh cilantro

SATAY AND SHISH KABOBS

The Filipino culture contains a rich mixture of ethnicities and their cuisines. The Indonesian connection is readily apparent in the popularity of satay. It consists of charcoal-grilled beef, chicken, mutton, tofu, or fish and is served on skewers. Satay can be prepared as an appetizer or served as a main course when accompanied by rice or a salad.

Satay is usually marinated in a thick coconut cream sauce flavored with various seasonings such as lemongrass, coriander, or peanut powder. The marinade is then used as a basting sauce while grilling.

Chicken Satay

Slice the chicken into ½ by 1 by 4-inch strips. Combine the garlic, curry, coriander, salt, butter, heavy cream, and coconut milk. Add the chicken strips to the mixture. Marinate at least 2 hours or overnight.

Soak 8-inch-long wooden or bamboo skewers in water for ½ hour just prior to using. Gather each chicken strip as if it were ribbon, and thread it onto a skewer. Continue the process until all the chicken is threaded onto skewers.

Basting with the remaining marinade, broil the satays 4 to 5 inches from the heat source or barbecue on the grill for 3 to 4 minutes. Turn the skewers over, and broil or grill for another 3 to 4 minutes, or until the chicken is well done. Serve immediately with the Curried Coconut Dipping Sauce (see recipe page 185).

2 pounds boned chicken breast

2 cloves garlic, minced

1 tablespoon curry powder

1 teaspoon ground coriander

1 teaspoon salt, or to taste

3 tablespoons butter, melted

3 tablespoon heavy cream

½ cup coconut milk

Tip: A simple but flavorful way to keep the grilled meat moist is to baste it, using a rosemary brush. To make one, cut large rosemary sprigs of the same size. Arrange the leaves to face one end. Tie the cut end with string to form a brush. The leaves retain the oils and marinades, as well as add flavor. Clean up couldn't be easier. When finished, just toss it away.

Curried Coconut Dipping Sauce

1 ¾ CUPS

This sauce has a piquant sweet/hot peanut taste just right for dipping. Coconut milk is available in Asian supermarkets.

Warm the peanut butter in the microwave for 20 seconds to soften. Whisk in the sugar. Gradually beat in the coconut milk or cream, lemon juice, curry powder, and chili hot sauce. Serve at room temperature.

2 tablespoons peanut butter

1 tablespoon raw or brown sugar

1 (15-ounce) can coconut milk or cream

1 teaspoon lemon juice

½ tablespoon curry powder

Dash chili hot sauce, optional

Chicken Satay Appetizers with Peanut Butter Yogurt Sauce

2 DOZEN

Soak 24 (8-inch-long) wooden or bamboo skewers in water for ½ hour just prior to using. Preheat the oven to 375° F. Lightly grease a 15 by 10 by 1-inch baking pan. Slice the chicken into lengthwise strips ½ inch wide. On each skewer, thread 1 piece green pepper, red pepper, and chicken strip. Place on greased pan.

In medium saucepan, combine the peanut butter, yogurt, soy sauce, cayenne pepper, and ¼ cup water; blend well. Remove ¼ cup of the sauce; brush on the chicken satay. Bake for 10 to 12 minutes, or until the chicken is no longer pink.

During the last minute of baking, heat the remaining sauce over low heat until hot, stirring occasionally. Serve as a warm dipping sauce with the chicken and pepper satays.

2 (2-pound) whole chicken breasts, skinned, boned, and split

1 medium green bell pepper, cut into 1-inch squares

1 medium red bell pepper, cut into 1-inch squares

½ cup creamy peanut butter

½ cup vanilla lowfat yogurt

2 tablespoons soy sauce

¼ teaspoon cayenne pepper, or to taste

Lemongrass Ginger Chicken Satay Appetizers

2 DOZEN

Lemongrass (tanglad) is an aromatic, lemon-scented grass that resembles a slim leek with a rounded stem and a layered stalk. Use only the lower 3 inches of the stalk for cooking. Lemongrass is available in Asian supermarkets.

Slice the chicken into lengthwise strips ½ inch wide. Place the chicken pieces in a large bowl. Combine the garlic, chili pepper, ginger, lemongrass, lime, coriander, sugar, turmeric, cumin, fennel, and salt, and rub into meat. Cover and refrigerate 4 to 24 hours.

While the chicken marinates, make the sauce. Soak 24 (8-inch-long) wooden or bamboo skewers in water for ½ hour just prior to using. Thread the chicken onto skewers. Brush the chicken with the peanut oil just before barbecuing or baking.

To barbecue: Grill 2 to 3 minutes on each side, or until the chicken is done and no longer pink. Serve piping hot with the Peanut Coriander Dipping Sauce.

To bake: Preheat oven to 375° F. Arrange skewers on baking sheets. Bake approximately 10 minutes, turning once, or until the chicken is done and no longer pink. Serve piping hot with the Peanut Coriander Dipping Sauce.

2 (2-pound) whole chicken breasts, skinned, boned, and split

2 cloves garlic, minced

1 small dried chili pepper, crushed, (¼ teaspoon) or to taste

1 (½-inch) slice fresh ginger, grated

1 stalk (3 inches) fresh lemongrass, minced, or 1 tablespoon dried

1 lime, juice plus zest

1 teaspoon ground coriander

1 tablespoon raw or brown sugar

½ teaspoon ground turmeric

½ teaspoon ground cumin

¼ teaspoon fennel seed

½ teaspoon salt, or to taste

Peanut Coriander Dipping Sauce (see recipe page 188)

2 tablespoons peanut oil

Peanut Coriander Dipping Sauce

2 CUPS

This dipping sauce works equally well with chicken, pork, or beef.

Heat oils in a saucepan. Sauté the onion and garlic until softened. Add vinegar and sugar, cooking until sugar dissolves. Remove from the heat and stir in the peanut butter, coriander, ketchup, soy sauce, lemon juice, and pepper. Serve dipping sauce at room temperature.

Tip: After making the dipping sauce, divide it into two bowls. Use one portion for basting, especially if grilling chicken or pork, and serve the other at the table alongside the satays.

4 teaspoons peanut or corn oil

2 teaspoons sesame oil

½ cup minced red onion

2 tablespoons minced garlic

1 tablespoon palm or red wine vinegar

1 tablespoon raw or brown sugar

⅓ cup peanut butter

½ teaspoon ground coriander

3 tablespoons ketchup

3 tablespoons soy sauce

1 tablespoon lemon juice

½ teaspoon ground white pepper, or to taste

Pork Satay with Brazil Nuts

20 TO 24 APPETIZERS

Serve this rich, nutty flavored satay as is or with any dipping sauce.

Cut the pork into strips the thickness, width, and length of bacon, ¼ by 1 by 8 inches. Set aside. In a large bowl, blend the ground nuts, coriander, red and black peppers, garlic, onion, salt, sugar, lemon juice, and soy sauce, and mix well. Add the pork strips to the marinade, mix well, cover, and refrigerate overnight or for a minimum of 2 to 3 hours.

Soak 8-inch-long wooden or bamboo skewers in water for ½ hour just prior to using. Gather each pork strip as if it were ribbon, and thread it onto a skewer. Continue the process until all the pork is threaded onto skewers. Broil the satays 4 to 5 inches from the heat source, basting with olive oil, for 3 to 4 minutes. Turn the skewers over, and broil for another 3 to 4 minutes, or until the pork is well done. Serve immediately.

1 ½ pounds lean pork

8 Brazil nuts, shelled and ground

2 tablespoons ground fresh coriander, or 1 teaspoon dried

⅛ teaspoon red pepper, or to taste

¼ teaspoon ground black pepper, or to taste

1 clove garlic, minced

2 tablespoons finely chopped onion

1 teaspoon salt, or to taste

1 tablespoon brown sugar

3 tablespoons lemon juice

¼ cup soy sauce

2 tablespoons olive oil

Broiled Pork Loin Satay

4 SERVINGS

This succulent pork kabob shows the Indonesian influence in the Philippines. Peanut butter, soy sauce, and curry combine a mouth-watering blend of flavors in both the marinade and dipping sauce.

Cut the pork into strips the thickness, width, and length of bacon, ¼ by 1 by 8 inches. Set aside. In a large bowl, blend the soy sauce and peanut butter. Stir in brown sugar, curry powder, lemon juice, red pepper, and garlic. Add the pork strips. Toss to coat both sides evenly. Cover and chill for overnight or for a minimum of 4 hours.

Soak 8-inch-long wooden or bamboo skewers in water for ½ hour just prior to using. Gather each pork strip as if it were ribbon, and thread it onto a skewer. Continue the process until all the pork is threaded onto skewers. Broil the satays 4 to 5 inches from the heat source for 3 to 4 minutes. Turn the skewers over, and broil for another 3 to 4 minutes, or until the pork is well done. Serve immediately with the Peanut Pepper Dipping Sauce (see recipe page 191).

1 ½ pounds pork loin

½ cup soy sauce

¼ cup creamy peanut butter

2 teaspoons brown sugar

2 teaspoons curry powder

2 tablespoons lemon juice

⅓ teaspoon crushed red pepper

1 clove garlic, minced

Peanut Pepper Dipping Sauce

³/₄ CUP

Combine the brown sugar, peanut butter, red pepper, garlic, and soy sauce.

1 tablespoon brown sugar

2 tablespoons
peanut butter

¹/₂ teaspoon crushed red
pepper

1 clove garlic, minced

¹/₂ cup soy sauce

Pork Loin Shish Kabobs

8 SERVINGS

Philippine cuisine has a wide variety of ethnic influences; one of them is American. Note the use of 7-Up among the traditional ingredients!

Chili peppers (sili) are available in two varieties: the longer siling mahaba and the smaller siling labuyo. Rule of thumb: the redder the color, the hotter the flavor. To reduce the heat yet retain the flavor of the chilies, remove the seeds and membranes.

Combine the meat with the pepper, soy sauce, vinegar, sugar, garlic, chili peppers, lemon juice, and 7-Up. Refrigerate and marinate for 8 hours or more, turning several times.

Soak 8-inch-long wooden or bamboo skewers in water for ½ hour just prior to using. Skewer the meat, alternating with the carrot pieces. Barbecue over a hot grill. Turning the skewers several times to ensure even heating, grill the shish kabobs for 12 to 15 minutes, or until the pork is white and thoroughly cooked. Serve with mounds of fluffy white rice.

2 pounds lean pork loin or shoulder, trimmed and cut into 1-inch cubes

1 tablespoon ground black pepper

1 cup soy sauce

1 cup vinegar

1 cup firmly packed raw or brown sugar

10 cloves garlic, minced

2 chili peppers, minced, or to taste

¼ cup fresh lemon juice

1 (12-ounce) can 7-Up

2 pounds carrots, peeled and cut into 1-inch lengths

8 cups cooked white rice

Beef Shish Kabobs

4 SERVINGS

Slice the onion into 8 wedges, and set aside. In a large bowl, combine the soy sauce, sugar, oil, coriander, and cumin. Stir in the sirloin and onion wedges. Cover and refrigerate for 1 hour.

Soak 8-inch-long wooden or bamboo skewers in water for ½ hour just prior to using. Remove the sirloin from the marinade, reserving the marinade. Alternating the sirloin cubes and onion wedges, thread them onto the skewers. Broil the shish kabobs 4 to 5 inches from the heat source for 3 to 4 minutes. Turn the skewers over, and broil for another 3 to 4 minutes, or until the beef is done to the desired degree.

1 medium Spanish onion

¼ cup soy sauce

2 tablespoons brown sugar

2 teaspoons vegetable oil

½ teaspoon ground coriander

½ teaspoon ground cumin

1 pound boneless sirloin, cut into 1-inch cubes

3 tablespoons smooth peanut butter

In small saucepan over medium heat, bring the reserved marinade to a boil. Whisk in the peanut butter and ⅓ cup water, stirring continuously for 1 to 2 minutes, or until thickened. Serve the shish kabobs steaming hot with the marinade-peanut mixture as a dipping sauce.

Barbecued Pork Shoulder Satay

8 SERVINGS

For this recipe to be authentic, the pork should marinate for 3 days—at room temper-ature! However, in the interest of safety, the directions have been somewhat modified. This version calls for the marinade to be refrigerated.

Cut the pork into strips the thickness, width, and length of bacon, ¼ by 1 by 8 inches. Set aside. Mix the remaining ingredients in a large bowl. Add the pork strips and stir to coat evenly. Cover, refrigerate, and marinate for 3 days, stirring occasionally.

Soak 8-inch-long wooden or bamboo skewers in water for ½ hour just prior to using. Gather each pork strip as if it were ribbon, and thread it onto a skewer. (Reserve the marinade.) Continue the process until all the pork is threaded onto skewers. Arrange the satays on the grill, and barbecue for 3 to 4 minutes. Turn the skewers over, and barbecue for another 3 to 4 minutes, or until the pork is browned and thoroughly cooked.

3 pounds pork boneless shoulder or loin roast

I cup vinegar

¾ cup barbecue sauce

I (12-ounce) can 7-Up

6 cloves garlic, minced

3 teaspoons salt, or to taste

I ½ teaspoons pepper, or to taste

I ½ cups sugar

To create a dipping sauce from the remaining marinade, bring it and ¼ cup water to a rolling boil in a 1-quart saucepan. Lower the heat, and simmer for 7 to 8 minutes, or until the sauce thickens.

Spicy Beef Kabobs

8 SERVINGS

Pork or chicken works equally well in this recipe. Experiment with all three, but if using pork be sure to cook it thoroughly.

Turmeric (dilaw) is a plant whose gingerlike root is ground into a spicy powder, used for flavoring and food coloring.

Mix the beef cubes with the cumin, cinnamon, coriander, turmeric, sugar, chili powder, salt, and vegetable oil. Cover, refrigerate, and marinate for 2 to 8 hours, stirring occasionally.

Soak 8-inch-long wooden or bamboo skewers in water for ½ hour just prior to using. Thread the beef onto 8 skewers. Arrange the shish kabobs on an aluminum foil-covered cookie sheet and broil for 3 to 5 minutes. Turn the shish kabobs over, and broil the other side for 3 to 5 minutes. Serve with sliced cucumbers and onions.

2 pounds beef,
cut into 1-inch cubes

1 teaspoon ground cumin

1 teaspoon ground
cinnamon

1 teaspoon ground
coriander

1 teaspoon ground turmeric

1 tablespoon raw or
brown sugar

½ teaspoon chili powder,
or to taste

½ teaspoon salt,
or to taste

2 tablespoons
vegetable oil

6 medium cucumbers,
thinly sliced

4 medium onions,
thinly sliced

Honey-Molasses Kabobs

4 SERVINGS

Use beef, pork, chicken breast, or veal, and marinate overnight in this sweet-sour sauce.

Combine the honey, molasses, soy sauce, vinegar, garlic, onion, salt, pepper, and meat. Cover and marinate overnight in the refrigerator.

Preheat to 350° F. Thread the meat cubes onto skewers, alternating with mushrooms and green and red peppers. Arrange skewers in a 9 by 13-inch pan. Brush the kabobs with the marinade, place in the oven, and bake for 10 to 15 minutes. Turn the kabobs and brush with the marinade again. Bake for an additional 10 to 15 minutes, or until the meat is done.

¼ cup honey

¼ cup molasses

¼ cup soy sauce

¼ cup wine vinegar

3 cloves garlic, minced

1 small onion, minced

1 teaspoon salt,
or to taste

½ teaspoon pepper,
or to taste

2 pounds boneless meat,
cut into 1-inch cubes

1 pound whole button
mushrooms

1 green pepper, cut into
eighths

1 red pepper, cut into
eighths

VEGETABLES

Because of their abundance and variety in the Philippines, vegetables are usually steamed and enjoyed for their natural flavor. Occasionally they are baked, grilled, broiled, sautéed, stir-fried, deep-fried, or pickled.

Cabbage, Philippine-Style

6 SERVINGS

Sauté the sausage, garlic, and onion over medium heat for 6 to 7 minutes, or until the sausage is thoroughly cooked. Add the cabbage to the sausage-onion mixture and stir-fry for 3 to 4 minutes, or until the cabbage is tender-crisp. Add the salt, pepper, and tomatoes during the last 2 minutes of cooking, stir-frying to heat evenly.

½ **pound lean pork sausage**

3 **cloves garlic, minced**

½ **cup coarsely chopped onion**

6 **cups shredded cabbage**

½ **teaspoon salt, or to taste**

¼ **teaspoon pepper, or to taste**

I **cup chopped tomatoes**

Baby Spinach in Coconut Milk

4 SERVINGS

To increase the heat of this dish, chop the habañera pepper before adding it to the recipe. A substitute for bagoong *is Korean* kimchi *or Japanese* miso. *Look for them in Asian supermarkets.*

Combine the coconut milk, pork, and ginger in a 2-quart saucepan. Bring to a boil, lower the heat, and simmer for 5 to 6 minutes, or until the pork is thoroughly cooked. Add the shrimp and *bagoong*. Simmer for an additional 5 to 6 minutes.

Add the pepper, coconut cream, baby spinach, salt, and pepper. Stirring occasionally, simmer for 2 to 3 minutes, or until the spinach is wilted. Serve hot.

1 1/2 cups coconut milk

1/2 cup minced pork

1 tablespoon minced ginger

4 medium shrimp, shelled, deveined, and minced

1 tablespoon *bagoong* (anchovy paste)

1 whole habañera pepper

1 (15-ounce) can coconut cream

1 pound baby spinach leaves, thoroughly rinsed

1/2 teaspoon salt, or to taste

1/4 teaspoon ground black pepper, or to taste

Spinach and Potatoes

4 SERVINGS

Serve this colorful vegetable side dish with either rice or freshly baked dinner rolls.

Heat the oil in a skillet over medium heat. Sauté the chopped onion until it becomes transparent. Add the chili peppers, stirring for 2 to 3 minutes, or until the peppers change color. Add the garlic, ginger, chili powder, salt. Sauté for 1 to 2 minutes. Fold in the dill and potatoes. Bring to a boil, reduce the heat, cover, and simmer for 8 to 10 minutes. When only a little water is left, add the spinach. Simmer for 5 to 6 minutes, or until the potatoes and spinach are tender. Remove from the heat, stir in the vinegar, and mix well. Transfer to a prewarmed platter, top with a pat of butter, and serve immediately.

2 tablespoons vegetable oil

1 medium onion, chopped

2 to 4 whole red chili peppers

4 cloves garlic, minced

2 tablespoons minced fresh ginger

½ teaspoon chili powder, or to taste

1 teaspoon salt, or to taste

¼ cup chopped fresh dill or 1 teaspoon dried dill weed

2 medium potatoes, cubed

1 pound fresh spinach, chopped

1 teaspoon palm or white vinegar

1 teaspoon butter

Eggplant Omelet

This recipe is delicious with any type of eggplants.

Boil the eggplants for 6 to 7 minutes, or until tender. Remove the skins. Set aside and keep warm.

Sauté the garlic, onion, ground pork, potato, and bell pepper until the vegetables are tender and the pork is thoroughly cooked. Season with salt and pepper, and keep warm.

Separate the egg whites from the yolks; beat the egg whites until stiff. Mix in the yolks. Heat 1 tablespoon oil in a skillet over medium heat. Spoon ⅛ of the beaten egg mixture into the skillet, and let it cook until it forms a crusty bottom. Place an eggplant on top of the egg. Lightly spread the pulp and top with ¼ of the pork-potato mixture. Add ¼ of the beaten egg mixture to the skillet. Carefully turn over the omelet to cook the topside. Repeat with the remaining eggplants, pork-potato mixture, and eggs.

4 Philippine eggplants

I tablespoon minced garlic

¼ cup diced onion

8 ounces ground pork

I medium potato, diced

¼ cup diced red bell pepper

**¼ teaspoon salt,
or to taste**

**⅛ teaspoon ground black
pepper, or to taste**

4 eggs

¼ cup vegetable oil

Filipino Salsa

2 CUPS

Combine all ingredients. Allow to rest at room temperature for 1 hour for the flavors to marry.

1 cup chopped fresh tomatoes

½ cup chopped onions

¼ cup grated radish

½ cup chopped fresh cilantro

½ teaspoon salt, or to taste

1 hot chili pepper, minced

2 tablespoons white vinegar or lime juice

Banana Wafers

4 SERVINGS

Plantains are considered a vegetable side dish when sliced and sautéed.

Remove the skin from the bananas and slice into ¼-inch-thick rounds. Heat the oil in a skillet and sauté the slices until crisp and golden. Remove from heat and arrange on paper towels to drain. Sprinkle liberally with salt and pepper and serve hot.

2 plantains or green bananas

¼ cup vegetable oil

½ teaspoon salt, or to taste

I teaspoon black pepper powder, or to taste

Baked Eggplant

GUINATAANY TALONG   **4 SERVINGS**

Philippine eggplants and coconut milk are available at Asian supermarkets.

Preheat the oven to 325° F. Using a fork, prick eggplants in several places. Roast in oven for 20 to 25 minutes, or until tender.

Meanwhile, sauté the onion in the oil in a nonaluminum skillet over low heat for 5 to 6 minutes, or until the onion is translucent. Peel the eggplants and mash the pulp. Fold into the onion. Add the vinegar, salt, pepper, and coconut milk. Stir constantly over low heat for 4 to 5 minutes, or until the flavors have married. Serve steaming hot.

4 Philippine eggplants

I medium onion, thinly sliced

2 tablespoons vegetable oil

2 tablespoons palm or white vinegar

½ teaspoon salt, or to taste

½ teaspoon ground black pepper, or to taste

I cup coconut milk

Filipino Refrigerator Pickles

3 CUPS

Nothing is as easy or refreshing on a hot summer's day than crisp, cool pickles, especially with this Filipino twist—tangy green papaya!

Blanch the papaya, green pepper, carrot, and *lasona* in boiling water for 1 minute. Drain and put into a large, clean bowl. In a nonaluminum pan, combine the vinegar, sugar, salt, and ginger. Bring to a boil, then pour over vegetables, and cool. Put into jars, cover, and store in the refrigerator for up to 1 week.

1 cup green papaya, sliced into ½-inch strips

1 green pepper, sliced into ½-inch strips

1 small carrot, sliced into ½-inch strips

1 bunch *lasona* (green onions) cut lengthwise

2 cups palm or apple cider vinegar

1 cup firmly packed raw or brown sugar

3 tablespoons salt, or to taste

1 (1-inch) piece ginger, shredded

Green Papaya Pickles

Measure grated papaya with a measuring cup and put into a clean bowl or a stainless steel saucepan. Add the salt and mix thoroughly. Cover the container and allow to stand overnight.

Place the grated papaya into a clean cloth or calico bag and squeeze out as much juice as possible. Spread the papaya thinly on drying trays or cookie trays and let dry for 1½ to 2 hours under the sun or inside a warm oven with the door ajar. Stir every 20 minutes to hasten drying.

Place the cloves and peppercorns in 2 small cloth bags. Boil the vinegars, seasoning bags, and sugar for 2 minutes. Add the ginger, onions, peppers, and grated papaya.

Stir well for 1 minute and pack into 2 clean, warm jars. Be sure the syrup covers the vegetables. Allow 1 seasoning bag per jar.

Seal tightly and refrigerate immediately. Keeps in refrigerator for up to 1 week.

Tip: For **Papaya Atsara**, the fruit should be immature and green in color. There should be no sign of yellow or red color on the skin, and the seeds should be white, not black.

2 green papayas, peeled and grated

1 teaspoon salt for each cup pickles, or to taste

1 teaspoon whole cloves

1 teaspoon black peppercorns

1 cup apple cider vinegar

½ cup white vinegar

1½ cups sugar

1 (3-inch) piece ginger, peeled and minced

2 medium onions, peeled and thinly sliced

2 sweet red peppers, julienned

DESSERTS

Fruit forms the basis of many native desserts in the Philippines: guava, jackfruit, star fruit, chico, sweetsop, mango, papaya, plantains, and various varieties of bananas. Of all the fruit, however, coconut is central to Filipino cuisine.

The Spanish introduced many baked goods and desserts to Filipino cuisine, among them flan, a popular egg custard. *Leche* is Spanish for "milk." *Leche* flan is a rich, velvety milk and egg-yolk custard, but sweeter, richer, and creamier than its original version.

Bibingka is a sweet, dense pancake with a slightly creamy consistency. It is usually made of sticky rice, but can be made from cassava or flour. In the Philippines, it is baked on a banana leaf. Toppings with contrasting flavors such as grated cheese, grated coconut, butter, or sugar are added during the final minutes of baking.

Simple and tasty, *torrones* are similar to banana fritters, but instead of batter, the banana spears are wrapped in egg-roll wrappers, sprinkled with brown sugar, and deep-fried to a golden brown. Serve with a scoop of rich vanilla ice cream.

Philippine Almond Float

Soften the gelatine in the cold water. Add the boiling water and sugar; stir until thoroughly dissolved. Pour in the milk and almond extract, mixing thoroughly. Pour into an 11 by 16-inch pan. Cover and refrigerate for 4 hours, or until set.

Cut into ½-inch cubes. Serve in chilled sherbet glasses with fruit cocktail and mandarin orange segments. Garnish with mint leaves.

5 envelopes Knox gelatine

1 cup cold water

2 ¼ cups boiling water

1 cup sugar

3 cup homogenized milk

3 teaspoons almond extract

1 cup chilled fruit cocktail

1 cup mandarin orange segments

8 sprigs fresh mint leaves

Sweet Rice

Filipino sweet rice is not only a traditional New Year's Eve treat; it is an easy-to-make dessert anytime. Malagkit, *coconut cream, and* mongo *are available in Asian supermarkets.*

Bring 2 cups water to a boil. Add the rice, cover, and simmer for 20 minutes, or until the water is absorbed.

Using a skillet, caramelize the brown sugar over medium heat for 1 to 2 minutes, and then add the coconut cream. Reserve ¾ cup of this mixture.

Add the rice to the brown sugar and coconut mixture. Stir frequently over medium heat until the rice is soft, 5 to 6 minutes. Spread on a cookie sheet.

2 cups *malagkit* or sweet rice

2 cups firmly packed brown sugar

1 (15-ounce) can coconut cream

1 cup *mongo* or mung beans

Boil the mung beans in ½ cup water for 5 to 6 minutes, or until tender. Drain thoroughly, and mash until the mixture is smooth.

Combine the mashed mung beans with the reserved brown sugar mixture in a saucepan. Stir constantly over medium heat until the mixture thickens. Spread on top of the rice and place under the broiler for 2 to 3 minutes, or until the top is a golden brown. Cut into squares and serve with ginger tea.

Tip: *Malagkit* or sweet rice is also known as glutinous rice, sticky rice, sushi rice, Chinese sweet rice, waxy rice, *mochi* rice, Japanese rice, and pearl rice. Despite its names, this rice is neither sweet nor glutinous. It is a sticky, short-grain rice widely used by Asians.

Flat Cake

BIBINGKA   15 TO 20 SQUARES

Traditionally the batter for flat cakes was poured into a banana leaf-lined clay dish and baked over charcoal. The cheese was made from the milk of water buffalos. However, what an aluminum cake pan, electric oven, and prepackaged cheese lack in local color, they make up for in convenience. Coconut milk is available in Asian supermarkets.

Preheat the oven to 375° F. Combine ¾ cup sugar with the coconut milk. Blend in the beaten eggs.

Combine the sifted flour, salt, and baking powder, and sift again. Fold in the egg mixture. Turn into a lightly greased 11 by 16-inch cake pan. Bake for 20 minutes. Sprinkle with the cheese, and bake for another 15 minutes, basting twice with the melted butter. Remove the cake from the oven, brush with the remaining butter. Sprinkle with the remaining ¼ cup sugar and the coconut. Slice into squares, and serve.

1 cup sugar

1¼ cups coconut milk

3 eggs, beaten

2 cups flour, sifted

½ teaspoon salt, or to taste

½ cup baking powder

½ cup grated Edam cheese

½ cup butter, melted

½ cup grated coconut

Tip: Because of its versatility and availability, coconut is widely used in Filipino foods. *Buko* or fresh young coconut produces a refreshing juice and sweet white flesh, while the mature coconut or *niyog* is grated and squeezed with water to make coconut milk or *gata*.

Bibingka II

Rice flour is available in Asian supermarkets.

Preheat the oven to 350° F. Sift the flour. Combine the butter with the sugar. Gradually add the flour, baking powder, milk, eggs, and vanilla, stirring constantly. Fold in the coconut. Pour the batter into a lightly greased 13 by 9-inch pan. Bake 1 hour, or until a toothpick inserted in the center comes out clean. When cool, cut into squares.

2 cups sweet rice flour

1 cup butter, softened

2 cups sugar

1 teaspoon baking powder

3 cups milk (fresh or evaporated)

5 eggs, beaten

1 teaspoon vanilla

1 cup grated coconut

Avocado Sundaes

4 SERVINGS

In the United States, avocadoes are relegated to the realm of salads and guacamole. However, in the Philippines, avocadoes are considered fruit and, as such, are sprinkled with sugar and eaten as a dessert. Try this subtle but amazingly flavorful combination.

Slice the avocadoes in half lengthwise and remove the seeds. Place the avocado halves on chilled dessert plates or in banana-split dishes. Place a scoop of vanilla ice cream in the center of each avocado half. Garnish with cherries.

2 large ripe avocadoes

1 pint vanilla ice cream

4 maraschino cherries

Coconut Pudding with Baked Bananas

4 SERVINGS

Coconut pudding is traditionally tinted with red food coloring to create a delightful pink hue. Top with toasted coconut for an unexpected crunch.

Combine the cornstarch, sugar, and ¼ cup coconut milk in a small bowl to form a smooth paste. In a saucepan, heat the remaining 1¼ cups coconut milk over medium heat for 1 to 2 minutes, or until just warm.

In a double boiler, combine the cornstarch paste and warm coconut milk, stirring constantly over medium heat until thick. Add the anise and food coloring; mix well. Pour into four custard bowls and chill for 2 hours, or until firm. Serve with the Baked Bananas (see recipe page 213). Garnish with toasted coconut.

3 tablespoons cornstarch

⅓ cup sugar

1½ cups coconut milk

1 teaspoon ground star anise

2 drops red food coloring, optional

2 tablespoons toasted coconut

Baked Bananas

4 SERVINGS

The Philippine Islands have many varieties of bananas: the saba *for cooking, the small sweet* latundan, *the larger exportable* bongolan, *the red-skinned* morado, *the seed-filled* Espanola, *the slim, finger-like* senoritas, *and the* saging. *Experiment with some of the more unusual varieties found in Asian supermarkets and notice the difference in taste, aroma, and texture.*

Preheat the oven to 400° F. Line a baking sheet with foil. Peel and slice the bananas into ¼-inch pieces. Spread out on the pan and brush with the butter. Bake for 13 to 15 minutes, or just until the bananas are soft. Spoon the hot baked bananas onto the chilled pudding (see recipe page 212) and serve immediately.

4 ripe bananas

2 tablespoons butter, melted

Sweet Bananas

In the Philippines, plantains or bananas are often considered a vegetable side dish, but substitute sugar for salt and the fruit becomes a dessert.

Combine the sugar and salt with 2 cups water. Bring to a boil, lower the heat, and simmer over medium heat until a thick syrup forms. Peel and slice the plantains thinly. Add the slices and butter to the syrup. Simmer gently for 8 to 10 minutes, or until the plantains are tender yet hold their shape. Spoon into stemmed goblets and serve hot. If desired, top with dark Filipino rum.

1 cup firmly packed dark brown sugar

¼ teaspoon salt, or to taste

4 plantains or bananas

½ cup butter

¼ cup dark rum, optional

Sweet Potato Dessert

4 SERVINGS

In the Philippines, sweet potatoes or yams are frequently served as dessert. Also called kumara, camote, *or* kamote, *sweet potatoes come in many colors, shapes, and sizes. At its simplest, boiled* camote *with a pat of butter is an easy snack, or try it mashed with milk and sugar. Thin slices can even be deep-fried and salted or sprinkled with confectioners' sugar to make* camote *chips. The following recipe raises this humble root to elegant new heights.*

Combine the sugar and salt with 2 cups water. Bring to a boil, lower the heat, and simmer over medium heat until it forms a syrup.

Peel and slice the sweet potato thinly. Add the slices and butter to the syrup. Simmer gently for 12 to 15 minutes, or until the sweet potato slices are tender, and the syrup thickens. Spoon into stemmed goblets and serve hot. If desired, top with dark Filipino rum.

I cup firmly packed dark brown sugar

¼ teaspoon salt, or to taste

I large sweet potato

½ cup butter

¼ cup dark rum, optional

Sweet Potato Fritters

Combine the flour, 2 tablespoons sugar, baking powder, and salt. Fold in the sweet potato slices and egg. Add the milk a tablespoon at a time. The batter should be thick enough to hold its shape. Heat the oil in a wok or deep pan. Form the batter into 2-inch balls and flatten into patties. Deep-fry in the hot oil for 1 to 2 minutes, or until the patties are golden, and the sweet potato slices are tender. Drain on paper toweling. Sprinkle liberally with sugar and serve piping hot.

I cup flour, sifted

I cup plus 2 tablespoons firmly packed raw or brown sugar

2 teaspoons baking powder

½ teaspoon salt, or to taste

I large sweet potato, peeled and thinly sliced (2 cups)

I egg, lightly beaten

3 to 4 tablespoons milk

I cup vegetable oil

Banana in a Blanket

TORRONES YIELDS 16

Simple and tasty, torrones *are similar to banana fritters, but instead of batter, the banana spears are wrapped in egg-roll wrappers, sprinkled with brown sugar, and deep-fried to a golden brown. Lumpia wrappers are available at Asian supermarkets, or you can make your own (see recipes page 108).*

Working with 1 lumpia wrapper at a time, place it on a clean surface. Slice each banana in half lengthwise, then crosswise to divide into fourths. Roll each banana piece in sugar and place it at the edge of the wrapper. Roll up the banana in the wrapper once, turn in edges, and continue rolling. Seal the open edge with a drop of water.

16 lumpia wrappers

4 bananas

¼ cup firmly packed raw or brown sugar

2 cups vegetable oil

Deep fry at 350° F for 3 to 5 minutes, or until golden brown. Drain on paper towels.

Tip: Serve warm with a scoop of rich vanilla ice cream.

Jackfruit Surprise

Jackfruit tastes like Juicyfruit gum. Try this mouthwatering blend of saba *bananas, jackfruit, and strawberries served with ice cream, home-made caramel sauce, and topped with chocolate filigree.* Saba *bananas,* langka, *and lumpia wrappers are available at Asian supermarkets.*

Cut the bananas into halves lengthwise; then cut each half into 4 strips lengthwise. Combine 1 cup of brown sugar with the bananas and *langka.* Place 1 lumpia wrapper on a plate. Arrange 4 strips of banana and some *langka* on each wrapper and wrap into a pouch. Tie top with a bit of string to close. Allow the wrapped bananas to rest on a platter at room temperature for 10 to 15 minutes, or until the wrappers absorb the sugar of the bananas.

Using a wok or 2-quart saucepan, deep-fry the wrapped bananas in hot oil for 2 to 3 minutes, or until the wrappers are golden brown. Remove with a slotted spoon and drain on paper towels.

Combine the cream, remaining 1-cup brown sugar, corn syrup, butter, vanilla, and salt in a saucepan. Stirring constantly, heat over medium heat until the mixture comes to a boil. Continue stirring for 2 minutes, or until the caramel sauce thickens. Remove from heat and cool.

Using a spoon, drizzle and swirl the melted chocolate onto wax paper, forming delicate patterns. Allow to set until cool. Use as a garnish.

Place the banana wrappers on 8 dessert plates. Divide the vanilla ice cream among the plates, and drizzle with caramel sauce. Garnish with fresh mint leaves, sliced strawberries, and the chocolate filigree.

4 *saba* bananas

2 cups firmly packed raw or brown sugar

½ cup ripe sliced *langka* (jackfruit)

8 round lumpia wrappers (see recipe page 108)

2 cups vegetable oil

1 cup light cream

1 cup corn syrup, light or dark

½ cup butter

1 teaspoon vanilla

¼ teaspoon salt, or to taste

4 ounces bittersweet chocolate, melted

1 pint vanilla ice cream

½ cup fresh mint leaves, optional

1 pint fresh strawberries, washed, hulled, and sliced

Chocolate Porridge

Champorrado *is a chocolate-flavored rice porridge that can be served for* almusal *(breakfast) or eaten later in the day as a snack. Enjoy this dish with a pinch of cinnamon.*

If using a rice cooker, add the rice and 1¼ cups water. Follow the rice cooker's directions. Once the rice begins to boil, add the condensed milk, cocoa mix, sugar, and ½ teaspoon cinnamon. Stir constantly to prevent rice from sticking to the bottom of the pot. If necessary, add another tablespoon water.

If steaming the rice, bring the rice and 1¼ cups water to a boil in a 2-quart pot. Lower the heat, cover, and simmer for 25 minutes. Once the rice begins to boil, add the condensed milk, cocoa mix, sugar, and ½ teaspoon cinnamon. Stir constantly to prevent rice from sticking to the bottom of the pot. If necessary, add another tablespoon water. Remove from the heat and allow to steam for 10 minutes.

I cup uncooked rice

½ cup sweetened condensed milk

3 packets instant cocoa mix (e.g., Carnation or Swiss Miss)

2 tablespoons sugar, or to taste

I teaspoon plus a dash cinnamon

I cup milk, optional

Serve with fresh milk, if desired, additional sugar, and a sprinkling of cinnamon.

Tapioca with Coconut Cream

Combine the tapioca with 6 cups water in a 3-quart saucepan. Bring to a boil, then lower heat, and simmer for 8 to 10 minutes, or until the tapioca becomes clear. Remove from heat, drain, and chill.

1 cup tapioca

1 (15-ounce) can coconut cream

2 cups prepared lemon gelatin, cubed

Dilute the coconut cream with 2 cups water. Stir the cream into the tapioca. Fold in the cubed gelatin, and serve in chilled dessert bowls.

Egg Balls

A simple but rich confection of sugar and eggs, Yema *is a Christmas Eve tradition in the Philippines.*

Simmer the milk over low heat until it is reduced to about 1 cup. Stir in sugar until dissolved. Remove from the heat and allow to cool slightly.

Mix 3 tablespoons of the warm simmered milk with the egg yolks. Gradually add this mixture to the milk in the saucepan, and simmer over low heat. Add the vanilla extract, and continue stirring until the mixture thickens. Remove from the heat and allow to cool to room temperature.

Shape the mixture into balls, rolling 1 tablespoon of the mixture into a ball. Dredge the finished balls in confectioners' sugar. For a festive presentation, serve each Egg Ball in a miniature soufflé cup or confection wrapper.

4 cups milk

¾ cup sugar

10 egg yolks

1 teaspoon vanilla extract

2 cups confectioners' sugar

Powdered Milk Candy

POLVORON   YIELDS ABOUT 30

Toast the flour in a saucepan over medium heat until a golden brown, stirring constantly to prevent scorching.

In a large bowl, combine the toasted flour, powdered milk, sugar, melted butter, and vanilla extract.

4 cups sifted cake flour

2 cups powdered milk

1 ½ cups sugar

¾ cup butter, melted

1 teaspoon vanilla extract

Mix well. Mold into oval, round, or more fanciful shapes. The texture is similar to marzipan. Present individually wrapped in colored Japanese paper or confection wrappers.

Mango Candy

YIELDS 15 TO 18

Combine the mango bits, condensed milk, and coconut. Shape into 1-inch balls, and roll in chopped nuts. Refrigerate for 2 to 3 hours, or until firm.

1 cup minced dehydrated mango

¾ cup sweetened condensed milk

2 ½ cups flaked coconut

1 cup almonds, finely chopped

Peanut Butter Candy

PASTILLAS DE MANI   36 PIECES

Combine the peanut butter, milk, and ¾ cup sugar in a saucepan. Stir constantly over medium heat for 2 to 3 minutes, or until the sugar has dissolved and the peanut butter has melted. Remove from heat.

1 ¼ cups peanut butter

1 cup milk

1 cup firmly packed raw or brown sugar

Sprinkle the remaining ¼ cup sugar onto a cutting board. When the candy mass is cool enough to handle, transfer it to the cutting board. Using a rolling pin, roll the candy to ½ -inch thickness. Slice the candy into ½ by 1-inch pieces. If necessary, dip the knife into water to make the slicing easier. Wrap the individual candies in waxed paper.

Cashew Candy

PASTILLAS DE CASOY   36 PIECES

Combine the cashews, condensed milk, lemon extract, and ¼ cup sugar in a saucepan. Stir constantly over medium heat for 2 to 3 minutes, or until the sugar has dissolved and the mixture forms a thick mass. Remove from heat.

1 ¼ cups chopped cashews

1 (8-ounce) can sweetened condensed milk

1 tablespoon lemon extract

½ cup firmly packed raw or brown sugar

Sprinkle the remaining ¼ cup sugar onto a cutting board. When the candy mass is cool enough to handle, transfer it to the cutting board. Using a rolling pin, roll the candy to ½-inch thickness. Slice the candy into ½ by 1-inch pieces. If necessary, dip the knife into water to make the slicing easier. Wrap the individual candies in waxed paper.

FLAN

Leche Flan

8 SERVINGS

Leche *is Spanish for the word* 'milk'. *Leche flan is a rich, velvety milk and egg-yolk custard.*

This creamy flan with its caramelized topping looks complicated but is a cinch to make. Try one or all of the following versions!

Preheat the oven to 325° F. Place ¾ cup sugar in a skillet. Heat over low heat. Watch very closely. As the sugar begins to melt, stir for 1 to 2 minutes, or until it is a golden brown. Stir continuously to avoid scorching. Pour the caramelized sugar into an 8-cup ring mold or divide among 8 custard cups.

1 ¼ cups granulated sugar

5 eggs

¼ teaspoon salt

1 teaspoon vanilla

3 ½ cups milk

In large bowl, whisk the eggs, remaining ½ cup sugar, salt, and vanilla for 1 to 2 minutes. Gradually add the milk, beating until smooth but not frothy. Pour into the ring mold or custard cups, over the caramelized sugar. Set the mold or cups into a pan of hot water 1 inch deep. Bake for 55 to 60 minutes, or until the custard sets.

Remove from the oven carefully. When the baking pans are cool enough to handle, carefully invert the flan onto a serving platter or individual dessert plates. Serve warm or chilled.

Lime Flan

Enjoy this rich and elegant dessert any time of the year.

Preheat the oven to 325° F. Place the sugar in a skillet. Heat over low heat. Watch very closely. As the sugar begins to melt, stir for 1 to 2 minutes, or until it is a golden brown. Stir continuously to avoid scorching. Pour the caramelized sugar into an 8-cup ring mold or divide among 8 custard cups.

1 cup granulated sugar

10 egg yolks

1 (8-ounce) can sweetened condensed milk

1 (5-ounce) can evaporated milk

Rind of 1 lime, grated

Using a fork, whisk the egg yolks, condensed milk, and evaporated milk with ½ cup plus 1 tablespoon water. Pour into the ring mold or custard cups, over the caramelized sugar. Sprinkle the grated lime rind on top. Making sure the water does not overflow into the custard, set the mold or cups on a wire wrack in a pan of hot water 1 inch deep, and steam for 1 hour, or until the custard is set.

Remove from the oven carefully. When the baking pans are cool enough to handle, carefully invert the flan onto a serving platter or individual dessert plates. Serve warm or chilled.

No-Bake Flan

This simplified flan recipe calls for cooking, not baking, and instead of caramelizing sugar for the topping, use dark corn syrup.

Drizzle the syrup into a fluted flan pan or 9-inch pie plate. Combine the egg yolks, condensed milk, evaporated milk, and sugar in a 1-quart saucepan. Stirring constantly over medium heat, allow the mixture to come to a full boil. Pour into the syrup-laced fluted flan pan or pie plate. Set until cooled to room temperature, and then refrigerate for 4 hours, or until set. When ready to serve, carefully invert the flan onto a serving platter.

½ cup dark corn syrup

8 egg yolks, lightly beaten

1 (8-ounce) sweetened condensed milk

1 (5-ounce) can evaporated milk

⅓ cup sugar

Sweet Potato Flan

Preheat the oven to 325° F. Over medium heat, constantly stir the sugar with 1 tablespoon water in a skillet or flan mold for 2 to 3 minutes, or until the sugar is caramelized. Coat the bottom of the flan mold evenly with the caramelized sugar. Set aside.

Combine the eggs, sweet potatoes, condensed milk, and vanilla thoroughly. Spoon the mixture on top of the caramelized sugar. Set the mold in a baking pan on the upper oven rack. Pour hot water around mold in pan to a depth of 1 inch. Bake, uncovered, for 50 to 55 minutes or until a knife inserted halfway between the center and edge comes out clean. Chill. Carefully loosen the custard from the sides and center of the mold; invert on a platter to serve.

¼ cup sugar

6 whole eggs, lightly beaten

¾ cup sweet potatoes, boiled and mashed

1 (8-ounce) can sweetened condensed milk

1 teaspoon vanilla extract

BEVERAGES

Excluding strictly Muslim areas, alcohol is part of the Filipino social scene. Native rums such as Tanduay are full-bodied, flavorful, and reasonably priced. The tropical climate is conducive to drinking beer; as a result, the local San Miguel beer is ubiquitous. The Philippine Islands are dotted with open-air beer gardens, often overlooking the ocean.

Several local brews are found in rural areas. *Tuba* (coconut wine) is prevalent in coconut-growing areas. Gatherers climb the coconut, buri, and nipa palm trees twice daily to collect sap from the cut tips of the growing trees. Gathered in bamboo tubes, the sweet sap becomes tart and alcoholic when fermented. In Laguna and Quezon, the sap is also distilled into *lambanog*, a high-proof liquor. In Northern Luzon, *tapuy*, rice wine, is brewed. The Kalingas and Ilocanos produce *basi*, a sugarcane wine, and Cebu and Ilocos are known for their grape vineyards and wine.

Nonalcoholic beverages are also popular, due to the hot climate. Fruit frappes and shakes made of green and ripe mango, papaya, melon, and avocado are refreshing on the hottest of days. At Christmastime, spicy ginger tea is a local favorite. Ginger tea is also considered a cold remedy and taken to ease congestion. And *tsokolate* (hot chocolate) is a universally popular breakfast drink.

Ginger Tea

Heat 4½ to 5 cups water with the ginger and brown sugar just until it comes to a boil. Reduce the heat and simmer for 15 to 20 minutes. Add more water to weaken the tea. Strain and serve hot or cold.

3 inches fresh ginger, thinly sliced

I cup firmly packed brown sugar

Sparkling Mango Sangria

2½ QUARTS

Reserve 3 lime and 3 carambola slices for garnish. In a large glass pitcher, combine the wine, nectar, mango, and remaining lime and carambola slices. Cover and chill overnight or for at least 1 hour. Just before serving, stir in the ginger ale, champagne, and ice cubes. Garnish with the reserved lime and carambola slices.

2 limes, thinly sliced

2 small carambolas (star fruit), thinly sliced crosswise

I chilled bottle dry white or rosé wine

I (12-ounce) can chilled mango nectar

I large mango, peeled, and cut into ½-inch cubes

I 12-ounce can chilled ginger ale

I bottle chilled champagne or sparkling wine

Melon Frappe

Combine the melon cubes, honey, and milk in a blender with 2 cups crushed ice. Using the pulse setting of the blender, blend for 1 minute, or until the mixture is frothy. Serve in chilled iced-tea glasses.

3 cups cubed honeydew or cantaloupe

½ cup honey, or to taste

1 cup milk

Tip: Thread melon cubes or balls onto wooden skewers and place in drinks as garnishes.

Ripe Mango Frappe

MANGGA FRAPPE   4 SERVINGS

Peel the mangoes, removing the flesh from the pit. Combine the mangoes and sugar with 4 cups crushed ice. Using the pulse setting of the blender, blend for 1 minute, or until the mixture is frothy. Serve in chilled iced-tea glasses.

4 medium ripe mangoes

½ cup sugar, or to taste

Tip: Thread mango cubes or balls onto wooden skewers and place in drinks as garnishes.

Variations:
Try these fruits in place of ripe mangoes:
Green Mango Frappe: 4 medium green mangoes.
Papaya Frappe: 1 large papaya.

Boracay Mango Shake

4 SERVINGS

Nothing is more refreshing than a mango shake on a hot summer's day. As you sip this frosty drink, close your eyes, sit back, and imagine you are beneath the palm trees on a tropical beach in Boracay, Philippines, enjoying the cool ocean breeze.

Peel the mangoes, removing the flesh from the pit. Combine the mangoes, sugar, and evaporated milk with 4 cups crushed ice. Using the pulse setting of the blender, blend for 1 minute, or until the mixture is frothy. Increasing the speed of the blender, blend for 1 minute, or until the mixture is creamy. Serve in chilled iced-tea glasses.

4 medium ripe mangoes

½ cup sugar, or to taste

1 cup evaporated milk

Variations:
Try these fruits in place of ripe mangoes:
Green Mango Shake: 4 medium green mangoes, peeled and cubed.
Pineapple Juice Shake: 4 cups freshly squeezed pineapple juice.
Fresh Pineapple Shake: 4 cups cut up pineapple. Reserve 4 spears for garnish.
Orange Shake: 4 cups freshly squeezed orange juice. Garnish with orange slices.
Papaya Shake: 1 large papaya, peeled and cubed.
Banana Shake: 4 medium bananas, peeled.

Tip: Add an ounce of Filipino rum to each serving for a tropical evening drink.

Rich Chocolate Drink

The cacao (Theobroma cacao) *tree, native to Central America, was introduced to the Philippines during the Spanish rule. It is widely cultivated, and it is no coincidence that chocolate is a Filipino favorite.*

Tsokolate *was once a mainstay at the Filipino breakfast table. Traditionally, the drink was prepared from fermented cacao seeds, which were sun-dried, roasted, pounded, and finally ground into a fine paste. The paste was then rolled into balls that hardened as they dried. These chocolate balls were scraped or shaved as needed. The following recipe contains a much easier method, using chocolate chips.*

Simmer the milk over medium heat in a large saucepan. Stir in the chocolate chips, and lower the heat, stirring constantly until the chocolate is melted. Whisk the egg yolks into the hot milk mixture, beating over low heat until the warm drink is frothy, usually about 2 to 3 minutes. Serve warm.

4 cups milk

2 cups semisweet chocolate chips

4 egg yolks, lightly beaten

Lemonade

CALAMANSI   8 SERVINGS

Pure calamansi *concentrate is available at local or online Filipino* sari-sari *(grocery stores), in the frozen food section. The* calamansi *is a small tropical fruit, similar to limes or lemons.*

Combine the frozen *calamansi* concentrate and sugar with 2 quarts cold water in a large pitcher. Stir vigorously until it is dissolved, and serve over ice.

6 ounces frozen *calamansi* concentrate or juice of 4 lemons

½ cup of sugar, or to taste

Sources for Filipino Ingredients

Alphabetical Listing of Filipino Markets

Following is a partial listing of grocery stores in the United States and Canada that carry an inventory of Filipino ingredients. Consult the Yellow Pages or search the web for more complete listings under *Groceries—Filipino*, *Groceries—Hispanic*, and *Groceries—Oriental*.

ALABAMA
Oriental Food Mart—2577 Madison Ave., Montgomery, AL (334) 263-7829

ARIZONA
Mabuhay Filipino Food Store—2023 S Craycroft Rd., Tucson, AZ (520) 747-2233
Manila Oriental Foodmart—3557 Dunlap Ave., Phoenix, AZ (602) 841-2977

CALIFORNIA
AJ's Bakery—914 E 8th St., Ste. 6, National City, CA (619) 477-8925
Alegria's Oriental Store—1601 Marine World Pkwy., Ste. 136, Vallejo, CA (707) 554-3835
Alice Cakeland—275 Quintard Ave., Chula Vista, CA (619) 425-8181
Alice Cakeland—3142 E Plaza Bl., #L, National City, CA (619) 479-3144
Anna's Oriental Grocery—61306 W Texas St., Fairfield, CA (707) 429-3106
Asian #1—4929 Mission St., San Francisco, CA (415) 584-4465
Asian Foods Etc—4375-J Clayton Rd., Concord, CA (510) 680-8828
Bataan Oriental Store—2706 Northgate Bl., Sacramento, CA (916) 923-5518
Beth's Oriental Store—1110 Marshall Rd., Unit 1, Vacaville, CA (707) 449-8332
Betsy Cake Center—8190-H Mira Mesa Bl., San Diego, CA (619) 271-1922
Betsy's Cake Center—1001 N Vermont Ave., Los Angeles, CA (213) 663-8634
Bingkahan At Iba Pa—18774 Amar Rd., Walnut, CA (818) 965-3080
Blimex Filipino Oriental Foods—3815 Railroad Ave., Pittsburg, CA (415) 432-4387
Bohol Market—1163 Venice Bl., Los Angeles, CA (213) 487-5757
Boracay Oriental Food Mart—1972 N Texas St., Ste. B, Fairfield, CA (707) 422-3663
CDC Trading—1201 Geneva Ave., San Francisco, CA (415) 587-0660
Cebu Oriental Foods—2312 Reo Dr., San Diego, CA (619) 475-0055

D'Executives Oriental Market & Video—1972 N. Texas St., Ste. B, Fairfield, CA (707) 422-3663

De Jesus Bake Shop—1840-C Coronado Ave., San Diego, CA (619) 424-3600

De Leon's Medical Clinic—255 E Maude Ave., Sunnydale, CA (408) 736-5147

Divisoria Food Mart—1061 E March Ln., Ste. A, Stockton, CA (209) 956-4602

DJ Oriental Market—14417 Roscoe Bl., Ste. D, Panorama City, CA (818) 892-4779

Eagle Rock Oriental Seafood Market—3756 W 40 Ave., Ste. N, Los Angeles, CA (213) 255-7827

ECM Oriental Market—11 Rancho Square, Vallejo, CA (707) 643-6904

Fajilan Oriental—691 Broadway Ave., Seaside, CA (408) 384-2019

Family Loompya—2720 Plaza Bl., National City, CA (619) 475-1025

Fiesta Market 500 W Willow St., Long Beach, CA (310) 426-9550

Fil-American Food Mart—1810 Colfax St., Concord, CA (415) 676-8453

Filipino Market—2569 Santa Fe Ave., Long Beach, CA (310) 426-3509

Filipino Store & Video—9522 Chapman Ave., Ste. B, Garden Grove, CA (714) 539-1158

Food Asia International Corp.—446 Cabot Rd., S San Francisco, CA (415) 873-6222

Gemely's Oriental Foodmart—1885 Contra Costa Bl., Pleasant Hill, CA (510) 686-9285

Goldilocks Bakeshops—17538 Pioneer Bl., Artesia, CA (310) 860-8286

Guia's Food Mart—104 Sunset Ave., Ste. H, Suisun City, CA (707) 426-6960

Handaan Grocery—5420 Mission St., San Francisco, CA (415) 334-7525

Happy Bakery—3142 E Plaza Bl., Ste. L, National City, CA (619) 479-3144

Iloilo Original Special La Paz Batchoy— 6055 Mission St., Daly City, CA (415) 584-2447

Ilonggo Delicacies—4710 Fountain Ave., Los Angeles, CA (213) 913-1939

Inang's Homemade Cuisine & Deli—6626 Mission St., Daly City, CA (415) 991-7244

Indian-Filipino Market—1906 Fremont Bl., Seaside, CA (408) 393-9175

Island Bakery—914 E 8th St., Ste. 6, National City, CA 91950 (619) 474-0600

Jesse's Bakeshop—12075 Carmel Mountain Rd., Ste. 207, San Diego, CA (619) 675-0633

Kabayan Bakery—222 E Plaza Bl., National City, CA (619) 470-7492

Kapitbahay Grocery Store—1201 Geneva Ave., San Francisco, CA (415) 587-0660

Kaunlaran Oriental Foods & Fish Market—12537 Alondra Bl., Norwalk, CA (310) 921-3215

Kay's Filipino Store & Video—4102 Orange Ave., Long Beach, CA (562) 596-9708

Laguna Seafood—4032 Eagle Rock Bl., Los Angeles, CA (213) 254-2634

Lechón ni Mang Tomas—15512 Cohasset St., Van Nuys, CA (818) 989-0065

Litson House—5142 Imperial Hwy., Lynwood, CA (310) 631-3211

Litson House—635 W Hueneme Rd., Oxnard, CA (805) 488-5343

Litson Station—1922 Willow St., Long Beach, CA (310) 424-5062

Little Quiapo Asian Food—753 Hickey Bl., Pacifica, CA (415) 359-7690

Luzon Foodmart—4502 Eagle Rock Bl., Los Angeles, CA (213) 259-2457

Mabuhay Oriental Foodmart—2610 S Bristol, Santa Ana, CA (714) 641-8631

Magat Asian Groceries & Trading—1873 Alvarado, Union City, CA
    (415) 487-1900

Magat Asian Groceries & Trading—14624 E 14th St., San Leandro, CA
    (510) 895-0477

Magat Asian Groceries & Trading—1188 Capitol Ave., San Jose, CA
    (408) 926-4412

Magat Asian Groceries & Trading—8102 Kelly Dr., N Stockton, CA
    (209) 952-3141

Magat Asian Groceries & Trading—772 Sandoval Way, Hayward, CA
    (415) 487-7244

Magat Asian Groceries & Trading—267 W Calaveras Bl., Milpitas, CA
    (408) 946-8583

Magat Mart—6 W Main St., Stockton, CA (209) 465-6565

Maharlika Food Market—87 Oriente St., Daly City, CA (415) 467-3933

Manila 99 Cents Minimart—502 Hoover, Los Angeles, CA (213) 662-6452

Manila Broiled Chicken—2026 Agnew Rd., Santa Clara, CA (408) 748-9110

Manila Food Festival—8018 E Santa Ana Canyon Rd, Anaheim, CA
    (714) 283-8690

Manila Meat Market—St. Francis Square, Daly City, CA (415) 991-7234

Manila Oriental Food Market—3323 Glendale Bl., Los Angeles, CA
    (323) 913-1380

Manila Grocery—23517 S Main St., Carson, CA (310) 830-6098

Maremy Oriental Foods—7993 Sierra Ave., Fontana, CA (909) 357-9311

Maricar's Bake Shop—920 N Citrus Ave., Covina, CA (818) 966-8795

Masagana Filipino Store—3019 Wilson Rd., Bakersfield, CA (805) 834-2511

Masagana Food Store—4253 W 3rd St., Los Angeles, CA (213) 384-1160

Maynila Seafood Market—17516 Pioneer Bl., Artesia, CA (310) 809-0554

MDC Sari-sari Store—4502 Eagle Rock Bl., Los Angeles, CA (213) 550-1825

Metro Manila Mart—13922 E Ramona Bl., Baldwin Park, CA (818) 337-8050

Minia's Bakeshop—36565 Newark Bl., Ste. K, Newark, CA (510) 791-8343

Nadel—914 E 8th St, Ste. 202, National City, CA 91950 (619) 336-1838

Naty's Food Market—6135 Mission St., Daly City, CA (415) 334-6685

Neslu Oriental—913 Cecil Ave., Delano, CA (805) 725-1654

New Manila Deli Phil Food Products—4506 Brookfield Dr., Sacramento, CA
    (916) 424-3563
Nora's Market & Video—3285 Willow Pass Rd., West Pittsburg, CA
    (510) 458-9539
Nora's Oriental Mart—795 Broadway, Seaside, CA (408) 899-7750
NTM Oriental—6277 Mission St., Daly City, CA (415) 756-8722
Oriental Food & Gift Mart—3428 Clayton Rd., Concord, CA (415) 680-6971
Oriental Food Center—1500 Sycamore Ave., B-6, Hercules, CA (415) 799-7808
Oriental Food Market—9180 Kiefer Bl., Sacramento, CA (916) 361-7120
Oriental Groceries—2148 Mission St., San Francisco, CA (415) 442-4949
Oriental Paradise Market—3403 E Plaza Bl., National City, CA 91950
    (619) 479-5190
Oriental Store of Fairfield—1926 N Texas St., Fairfield, CA (707) 427-0393
Oriental Store of Vallejo—962 Adm Callaghan Ln., Vallejo, CA (707) 552-6800
Pacific Filipino Oriental Store—2254 Pacific Ave., Long Beach, CA
    (562) 591-7599
Pag-Asa Foods—1557 E Amar Rd., Unit K, W Covina, CA (818) 965-6828
Pampanga Foods Corp.—1835 Orangethorpe Park, Anaheim, CA
    (714) 778-8800
Phil Food Mart—125 Sun St., Salinas, CA (408) 292-5377
Phil Mart Grocery & Bake Shop—950 King Dr., Ste. 109, Daly City, CA
    (415) 878-1611
Phil Oriental Mart—21720 S Vermont, Ste. 106, Torrance, CA (310) 328-9010
Phil-Am Mart—4330 E 14th St., Oakland, CA (510) 261-1357
Phil-Asian Discount Food Market—2930 Beverly Bl., Los Angeles, CA
    (213) 383-7713
Phil-Mart—950 King Dr., Ste. 109, Daly City, CA (415) 878-1611
Philhouse Seafood Market—810 Nogales St., Walnut, CA (818) 810-1880
Philippine Delicacies & Foodmart—5609 Mission St., San Francisco, CA
    (415) 239-8554
Philippine Grocery—34 Woodward, San Francisco, CA (415) 552-6774
Philippine Grocery—92 Hill St., Daly City, CA (415) 991-2043
Philippine Grocery—4929 Mission St., San Francisco, CA (415) 584-4465
Philippine Grocery—3837 Sonoma Bl., Vallejo, CA (707) 554-3297
Philippine Grocery—34601 Alvarado Niles St., Union City, CA (415) 471-1036
Philippine Grocery—8th St., San Francisco, CA (415) 626-3734
Pilipinas Bakery—3640 Saviers Rd., Oxnard, CA (805) 486-3878
Pinoy Mini Mart—2223 Colorado Bl., Los Angeles, CA (213) 256-4920
Pioneer Oriental Mart—18819 Pioneer Bl., Artesia, CA (310) 865-4192
Rainbaird Manila Bakery—16028 E Amar Rd., City of Industry, CA
    (818) 968-0890

Red Ribbon Bake Shop—1420 E Plaza Bl., National City, CA (619) 477-5897

Red Ribbon Bakeshop—11900 South St., #105, Cerritos, CA (562) 402-3304

Red Ribbon Bakeshop—3550 Carson St., #402, Torrance, CA (310) 542-1991

Red Ribbon Bakeshop—1115 Centre Dr., City of Industry, CA (909) 598-1586

Red Ribbon Bakeshop—1225 Amar Rd., W Covina, CA (626) 964-2419

Red Ribbon Bakeshop—6091 Sunset Bl., Los Angeles, CA (213) 465-5999

Rene's Bakery—32122 Alvarado Bl., Union City, CA (510) 429-1288

Rene's Oriental Market—2736 35th Ave., Oakland, CA (510) 534-9351

RNJ Oriental Mart—310 N Citrus Ave., Unit L, Azusa, CA (818) 969-7468

Rose Empanada & Specialties—40 San Pedro, Daly City, CA (415) 992-1611

S & D Oriental Market—400 Moffett Bl., Ste. G, Mountain View, CA
    (415) 964-5080

Sari-sari Oriental Foods—26234 Bouquet Canyon Rd., Sangus, CA (805) 253-
    5052

Sari-sari Store—160 Leland Ave., Ste. A, San Francisco, CA (415) 239-0580

Seafood City Supermarket—3660 S Nogales St., West Covina, CA
    (626) 964-4121

Tambuli Oriental Market—124-126 W Carson St., Carson, CA
    (310) 549-4251

Toto's Lechón—1545E Amar Rd., W Covina, CA (818) 810-5266

Toto's Lechón—4110 Verdugo Rd., Los Angeles, CA (213) 259-9926

U-Need Oriental Store—623 Caliente Dr., Sunnyvale, CA (408) 730-9640

Valerio City Bakery—1631 E. 8th St., National City, CA (619) 477-8588

Valerio's Bakery—2518 Berryessa Rd., San Jose, CA (408) 254-9490

Valerio's Tropical Bakeshop—3718 Sonoma Bl., Vallejo, CA (707) 552-6636

Valerio's Tropical Bakeshop—950 King Dr., Suite 107, Daly City, CA
    (415) 868-1611

Vanessa's Oriental Market & Video—255 E Maude Ave., Sunnyvale, CA
    (408) 736-5147

Vien-Dong III—6935 Linda Vista Rd, San Diego, CA (619) 292-7176

Vierneza Filipino Store—2477 San Bruno Ave., San Francisco, CA
    (415) 468-1346

Viray Asian Grocery and Trading—27098 Hesperian Bl., Hayward, CA
    (415) 887-1325

Western Pacific Oriental Grocery—905 E Duane Ave., Sunnyvale, CA
    (408) 720-1006

CONNECTICUT

Fil Asian Foods—1127 Main St., Hartford, CT (203) 291-8727

ILLINOIS

Oriental Food Mart—Westlake Plaza, 2208 Bloomingdale Rd., Glendale
    Heights, IL (312) 980-1779
Philippine Food Corp—4547 N. Ravenswood, Chicago, IL (312) 784-7447
Philippine World—1051-57 W. Belmont Ave., Chicago, IL (312) 248-5100

MARYLAND

Asian American Grocery Store—5808 Riggs Rd., Hyattsville, MD
    (301) 559-6060
Asian Village International Supermarket—2101 University Bl., Hyattsville,
    MD (301) 422-2511
Halina Oriental Store—5846 Allentown Way, Camp Springs, MD
    (301) 449-5117
Salinas Oriental Store—9205 Oxon Hill Rd., Ft. Washington, MD
    (301) 567-2732

MASSACHUSETTS

Oriental Giftland—72 Harrison Avenue, Boston, MA (617) 426-0773

MICHIGAN

Oriental Food Groceries—18919 W. Seventh Mile, Detroit, MI (313) 534-7773
Phil-Asian Tropical Food Mart—4638 Woodward, Detroit, MI (313) 831-7530

MINNESOTA

Phil-Oriental Imports, Inc.—476 Lexington Pkwy., St. Paul MN (612) 646-5479

NEVADA

Manila Grocery—3465 Lake Tahoe Bl., S Lake Tahoe, NV (916) 542-0919
Nita's Oriental—1515 4th St., Sparks, NV (702) 355-0150

NEW JERSEY

Alex's Filipino Store—326 North Ave., Box 213, Dunellen, NJ (908) 968-9685
American Pinoy Foodmart—1347 Kennedy Bl., Bayonne, NJ (201) 436-7587
American Pinoy Supermarket—108 S Front St., Bergenfield, NJ (201) 387-7979
Arctic Food/Asian Group—Morris Ave., Union, NJ (908) 281-8051
    Visit web site: http://www.angelfire.com/nj/bathan
    or send e-mail to: foodex@hotmail.com
Asia Oriental Food & Gifts—256 Rt. 46, Dover, NJ (201) 366-0289
Asian Food—217 Summit Ave., Jersey City, NJ (201) 333-7254
Asian Food Center—1723 Rt. 27 Tops Plaza, Edison, NJ (908) 819-8139
Fil-Orient Foodmart—472 West Side Ave., Jersey City, NJ (201) 435-6716

Filipinas Grocery & Deli—93 Bowers St., Jersey City, NJ (201) 792-7072

Filipino Family Foodmart—469 Main St., Orange, NJ (201) 674-7242

Filmart—173 Stelton Rd., Piscataway, NJ—(908) 752-4977

Great Pacific Oriental Products—405 Bloomfield Ave., Caldwell, NJ
(201) 403-0071

Jollibee Oriental Store—48 E Main St., Bergenfield, NJ (201) 439-1242

Jun's Grocery— 432 West Side Ave., Jersey City, NJ (201) 333-6944

Jersey Oriental Foodtown—530-A Newark Ave., Jersey City, NJ
(201) 659-1933

Maharlika Orient—128 Main Ave., Passaic Park, NJ (201) 778-7790

Manila Meat Distributors—101 Summit Ave., Jersey City, NJ (201) 792-7156

Manila Mini Mart—473 Mercer St., Jersey City, NJ (201) 451-5576

Ocampo's Fil-Am Deli Store—128 W Main St., Bergenfield, NJ
(201) 385-9519

Phil-Am Foodmart Inc.—324 Hoboken Ave., Jersey City, NJ (201) 963-0455

Philippine Bread House—530 Newark Ave., Jersey City, NJ (201) 659-1753

Philtrade Food Center—231 Main Ave., Passaic Park, NJ (201) 773-4755

RD's Sari-sari Store—178 Franklin St., Belleville, NJ (201) 450-8441

Sampaguita Foodmart—115 Bowers St., Jersey City, NJ (201) 659-5233

Sunrise Oriental Products—253 Main St., Hackensack, NJ (201) 487-8996

NEW YORK

Asia Food Market—71 1/2 Mulberry St., New York, NY (212) 962-2020

Asian Best—Middle Country Rd., Centereach, NY (516) 732-7336

Dayleg Fil-Mart—3555 Victory Bl., Staten Island, NY (718) 370-1746

F&D Oriental Food Mart—104 St. Nicholas Ave., Brooklyn, NY (718) 497-6545

Goodland Health & Oriental Grocery—255-21 Hillside Ave., Floral Park, NY
(718) 347-8312

Kam Lun Food Products, Inc.—86-8 Broadway, Elmhurst, NY (718) 446-9720

Mabuhay Silangan Store—6906 Roosevelt Ave., Woodside, NY (718) 651-7298

Manila Food-O-Rama—3348 Long Beach Rd., Oceanside, NY (516) 678-1122

Manila-Asia Variety—68-70 Belmont Ave., Belleville, NY (201) 751-7556

Manny's Bake Shop—8269 Parson Bl., Jamaica Hill, Queens, NY (718) 380-0802

Masagana Oriental Foodmart—18716 Hillside, Hollis, NY (718) 217-0120

New Manila Foodmart—351 E 14th St., New York, NY (212) 480-8182

Pearl-Orient Foods—75 Atlantic Ave., Brooklyn, NY (718) 875-4435

Phil-Am Foods of Staten—527 Tompkins Ave., Staten Island, NY (718) 876-6948

Phil-Thai Grocery—2924 36th Ave., Astoria, NY (718) 392-5512

Philippine Bread House—30-93 37th St., Astoria, NY (718) 267-1534

Sari-sari—87-16 Parsons Bl., Jamaica, NY (718) 658-4335

United Filipino Foods—3093 37th St., Astoria, NY (718) 267-1534

OHIO

Bayanihan Food, Inc.—625 Bolivar, Cleveland, OH (216) 781-2468

OKLAHOMA

Mabuhay Philippines—416 SW Lee Bl., Lawton, OK (580) 248-4567

PENNSYLVANIA

Phil-Am Food Mart—5601 Camac, Philadelphia, PA (215) 927-7373

TEXAS

Little Home Bakery & Grocery—2109 Parker Rd., Ste. 202A, Plano, TX (214) 596-3382

VIRGINIA

Angie's Bakery—3502 Holland Rd., #102, Virginia Beach, VA (804) 431-2070

Apsara Oriental Food Market—291 Sunset Park Dr., Hemdon, VA (703) 471-9194

Bayanihan Oriental Store—12710 Darby Brooke Ct., Lake Ridge, VA (703) 490-1972

D&V Oriental Bakery & Grocery—1400 Kempsville Rd., Ste. 130, Chesapeake, VA (804) 548-4605

Fiesta Oriental Store—4915 1st St., Arlington, VA (703) 515-9160

Filipino Oriental Store—3016-B Franklin Rd., Roanoke, VA (703) 981-0981

Freddie's Seafood & Oriental Store—8509 Hampton Bl., Norfolk, VA (804) 489-0081

Laguna Bakery—1255 Fordham Dr., Ste. 108, Virginia Beach, VA (804) 366-0704

Lita's Oriental Food Mart—1128 Green Run Sq., Virginia Beach, VA (804) 427-5786

Mabuhay Oriental Store—6615 Backlick Rd., Springfield, VA (703) 451-8986

Maggie's Bake Shop—4809 N First St., Arlington, VA (703) 276-2898

Maharlika Oriental Store—6365 Livingston Rd., #108, Virginia Beach, VA (301) 567-8288

Maymar International Food Mart—5347 Lila Ln., Virginia Beach, VA (804) 420-9788

Meng oriental Store—1630 General Booth Bl., 109, Virginia Beach, VA (804) 721-3154

Mercy Oriental Food—7824 Gifford St., Norfolk, VA (804) 588-7087

Oriental Express Groceries—1512 Lynnhaven Pkwy., Virginia Beach, VA (804) 471-7237

Phil-Asian Food Mart—14511-Q Lee Jackson Memor. Hwy., Chantilly, VA (703) 263-2769

Philippine Oriental Market & Carry Out—3610 Lee Hwy., Arlington, VA
(703) 528-0300

Remy's Fish & Seafood—13602 Bottner Ct., Woodbridge, VA (703) 490-6742

Remy's Puto & Kutchinta—13602 Bottner Ct., Woodbridge, VA (703) 490-6742

Reyes Seafood—352 Cleveland pl., #109, Virginia Beach, VA (804) 456-5609

Sally's Bakery & Grocery—4221 Pleasant Valley Rd., Ste. 129, Virginia Beach,
VA (804) 467-7461

WASHINGTON

Fiesta Filipina Store—522 6th South, Seattle, WA (206) 624-6160

CANADA

Filipino Market—4 Irwin Ave., Toronto, Ontario, Canada (416) 967-6532

Philippine Products Sari-Sari Store—507-B Gladstone Ave., Ottawa, Ontario,
Canada

Philippine Sari-Sari Store—4939 Cote des Neiges, Montreal, Quebec, Canada

Web Listing of Filipino Markets

If no Filipino, Hispanic, or Oriental grocery store is nearby, consider having
the ingredients shipped from a cyber Filipino grocery store. Using a search
engine on the web, type in groceries + Filipino + online, or groceries + Hispanic + online, or groceries + Oriental + online. Following are several links
to cyber grocery stores that carry and ship Filipino ingredients:

http://www.pilipinomart.com/
http://www.filipinolinks.com/business/groceries.html
http://www.sarisaristore.net/prod03.phtml
http://www.sari-cyberstore.com/
http://www.orientalfoodexpress.com/
http://www.bonelessbangus.com/
http://fitrite.hypermart.net/
http://www.hwanam.com/
http://www.pinoydelikasi.com/main.php
http://www.orientalfoodstore.com/

INDEX